FREE Test Taking Tips DVD Offer

To help us better serve you, we have developed a Test Taking Tips DVD that we would like to give you for FREE. **This DVD covers world-class test taking tips that you can use to be even more successful when you are taking your test.**

All that we ask is that you email us your feedback about your study guide. Please let us know what you thought about it – whether that is good, bad or indifferent.

To get your **FREE Test Taking Tips DVD**, email freedvd@studyguideteam.com with "FREE DVD" in the subject line and the following information in the body of the email:

a. The title of your study guide.

b. Your product rating on a scale of 1-5, with 5 being the highest rating.

c. Your feedback about the study guide. What did you think of it?

d. Your full name and shipping address to send your free DVD.

If you have any questions or concerns, please don't hesitate to contact us at freedvd@studyguideteam.com.

Thanks again!

Praxis English Language Arts Content Knowledge Study Guide

Praxis 5038 Study Guide & Practice Test Questions
[3rd Edition]

TPB Publishing

Interested in buying more than 10 copies of our product? Contact us about bulk discounts:
bulkorders@studyguideteam.com

ISBN 13: 9781628458893
ISBN 10: 1628458895

.

Table of Contents

Quick Overview

As you draw closer to taking your exam, effective preparation becomes more and more important. Thankfully, you have this study guide to help you get ready. Use this guide to help keep your studying on track and refer to it often.

This study guide contains several key sections that will help you be successful on your exam. The guide contains tips for what you should do the night before and the day of the test. Also included are test-taking tips. Knowing the right information is not always enough. Many well-prepared test takers struggle with exams. These tips will help equip you to accurately read, assess, and answer test questions.

A large part of the guide is devoted to showing you what content to expect on the exam and to helping you better understand that content. In this guide are practice test questions so that you can see how well you have grasped the content. Then, answer explanations are provided so that you can understand why you missed certain questions.

Don't try to cram the night before you take your exam. This is not a wise strategy for a few reasons. First, your retention of the information will be low. Your time would be better used by reviewing information you already know rather than trying to learn a lot of new information. Second, you will likely become stressed as you try to gain a large amount of knowledge in a short amount of time. Third, you will be depriving yourself of sleep. So be sure to go to bed at a reasonable time the night before. Being well-rested helps you focus and remain calm.

Be sure to eat a substantial breakfast the morning of the exam. If you are taking the exam in the afternoon, be sure to have a good lunch as well. Being hungry is distracting and can make it difficult to focus. You have hopefully spent lots of time preparing for the exam. Don't let an empty stomach get in the way of success!

When travelling to the testing center, leave earlier than needed. That way, you have a buffer in case you experience any delays. This will help you remain calm and will keep you from missing your appointment time at the testing center.

Be sure to pace yourself during the exam. Don't try to rush through the exam. There is no need to risk performing poorly on the exam just so you can leave the testing center early. Allow yourself to use all of the allotted time if needed.

Remain positive while taking the exam even if you feel like you are performing poorly. Thinking about the content you should have mastered will not help you perform better on the exam.

Once the exam is complete, take some time to relax. Even if you feel that you need to take the exam again, you will be well served by some down time before you begin studying again. It's often easier to convince yourself to study if you know that it will come with a reward!

Test-Taking Strategies

1. Predicting the Answer

When you feel confident in your preparation for a multiple-choice test, try predicting the answer before reading the answer choices. This is especially useful on questions that test objective factual knowledge. By predicting the answer before reading the available choices, you eliminate the possibility that you will be distracted or led astray by an incorrect answer choice. You will feel more confident in your selection if you read the question, predict the answer, and then find your prediction among the answer choices. After using this strategy, be sure to still read all of the answer choices carefully and completely. If you feel unprepared, you should not attempt to predict the answers. This would be a waste of time and an opportunity for your mind to wander in the wrong direction.

2. Reading the Whole Question

Too often, test takers scan a multiple-choice question, recognize a few familiar words, and immediately jump to the answer choices. Test authors are aware of this common impatience, and they will sometimes prey upon it. For instance, a test author might subtly turn the question into a negative, or he or she might redirect the focus of the question right at the end. The only way to avoid falling into these traps is to read the entirety of the question carefully before reading the answer choices.

3. Looking for Wrong Answers

Long and complicated multiple-choice questions can be intimidating. One way to simplify a difficult multiple-choice question is to eliminate all of the answer choices that are clearly wrong. In most sets of answers, there will be at least one selection that can be dismissed right away. If the test is administered on paper, the test taker could draw a line through it to indicate that it may be ignored; otherwise, the test taker will have to perform this operation mentally or on scratch paper. In either case, once the obviously incorrect answers have been eliminated, the remaining choices may be considered. Sometimes identifying the clearly wrong answers will give the test taker some information about the correct answer. For instance, if one of the remaining answer choices is a direct opposite of one of the eliminated answer choices, it may well be the correct answer. The opposite of obviously wrong is obviously right! Of course, this is not always the case. Some answers are obviously incorrect simply because they are irrelevant to the question being asked. Still, identifying and eliminating some incorrect answer choices is a good way to simplify a multiple-choice question.

4. Don't Overanalyze

Anxious test takers often overanalyze questions. When you are nervous, your brain will often run wild, causing you to make associations and discover clues that don't actually exist. If you feel that this may be a problem for you, do whatever you can to slow down during the test. Try taking a deep breath or counting to ten. As you read and consider the question, restrict yourself to the particular words used by the author. Avoid thought tangents about what the author *really* meant, or what he or she was *trying* to say. The only things that matter on a multiple-choice test are the words that are actually in the question. You must avoid reading too much into a multiple-choice question, or supposing that the writer meant something other than what he or she wrote.

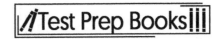

5. No Need for Panic

It is wise to learn as many strategies as possible before taking a multiple-choice test, but it is likely that you will come across a few questions for which you simply don't know the answer. In this situation, avoid panicking. Because most multiple-choice tests include dozens of questions, the relative value of a single wrong answer is small. As much as possible, you should compartmentalize each question on a multiple-choice test. In other words, you should not allow your feelings about one question to affect your success on the others. When you find a question that you either don't understand or don't know how to answer, just take a deep breath and do your best. Read the entire question slowly and carefully. Try rephrasing the question a couple of different ways. Then, read all of the answer choices carefully. After eliminating obviously wrong answers, make a selection and move on to the next question.

6. Confusing Answer Choices

When working on a difficult multiple-choice question, there may be a tendency to focus on the answer choices that are the easiest to understand. Many people, whether consciously or not, gravitate to the answer choices that require the least concentration, knowledge, and memory. This is a mistake. When you come across an answer choice that is confusing, you should give it extra attention. A question might be confusing because you do not know the subject matter to which it refers. If this is the case, don't eliminate the answer before you have affirmatively settled on another. When you come across an answer choice of this type, set it aside as you look at the remaining choices. If you can confidently assert that one of the other choices is correct, you can leave the confusing answer aside. Otherwise, you will need to take a moment to try to better understand the confusing answer choice. Rephrasing is one way to tease out the sense of a confusing answer choice.

7. Your First Instinct

Many people struggle with multiple-choice tests because they overthink the questions. If you have studied sufficiently for the test, you should be prepared to trust your first instinct once you have carefully and completely read the question and all of the answer choices. There is a great deal of research suggesting that the mind can come to the correct conclusion very quickly once it has obtained all of the relevant information. At times, it may seem to you as if your intuition is working faster even than your reasoning mind. This may in fact be true. The knowledge you obtain while studying may be retrieved from your subconscious before you have a chance to work out the associations that support it. Verify your instinct by working out the reasons that it should be trusted.

8. Key Words

Many test takers struggle with multiple-choice questions because they have poor reading comprehension skills. Quickly reading and understanding a multiple-choice question requires a mixture of skill and experience. To help with this, try jotting down a few key words and phrases on a piece of scrap paper. Doing this concentrates the process of reading and forces the mind to weigh the relative importance of the question's parts. In selecting words and phrases to write down, the test taker thinks about the question more deeply and carefully. This is especially true for multiple-choice questions that are preceded by a long prompt.

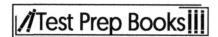

9. Subtle Negatives

One of the oldest tricks in the multiple-choice test writer's book is to subtly reverse the meaning of a question with a word like *not* or *except*. If you are not paying attention to each word in the question, you can easily be led astray by this trick. For instance, a common question format is, "Which of the following is…?" Obviously, if the question instead is, "Which of the following is not…?," then the answer will be quite different. Even worse, the test makers are aware of the potential for this mistake and will include one answer choice that would be correct if the question were not negated or reversed. A test taker who misses the reversal will find what he or she believes to be a correct answer and will be so confident that he or she will fail to reread the question and discover the original error. The only way to avoid this is to practice a wide variety of multiple-choice questions and to pay close attention to each and every word.

10. Reading Every Answer Choice

It may seem obvious, but you should always read every one of the answer choices! Too many test takers fall into the habit of scanning the question and assuming that they understand the question because they recognize a few key words. From there, they pick the first answer choice that answers the question they believe they have read. Test takers who read all of the answer choices might discover that one of the latter answer choices is actually *more* correct. Moreover, reading all of the answer choices can remind you of facts related to the question that can help you arrive at the correct answer. Sometimes, a misstatement or incorrect detail in one of the latter answer choices will trigger your memory of the subject and will enable you to find the right answer. Failing to read all of the answer choices is like not reading all of the items on a restaurant menu: you might miss out on the perfect choice.

11. Spot the Hedges

One of the keys to success on multiple-choice tests is paying close attention to every word. This is never truer than with words like almost, most, some, and sometimes. These words are called "hedges" because they indicate that a statement is not totally true or not true in every place and time. An absolute statement will contain no hedges, but in many subjects, the answers are not always straightforward or absolute. There are always exceptions to the rules in these subjects. For this reason, you should favor those multiple-choice questions that contain hedging language. The presence of qualifying words indicates that the author is taking special care with his or her words, which is certainly important when composing the right answer. After all, there are many ways to be wrong, but there is only one way to be right! For this reason, it is wise to avoid answers that are absolute when taking a multiple-choice test. An absolute answer is one that says things are either all one way or all another. They often include words like *every*, *always*, *best*, and *never*. If you are taking a multiple-choice test in a subject that doesn't lend itself to absolute answers, be on your guard if you see any of these words.

12. Long Answers

In many subject areas, the answers are not simple. As already mentioned, the right answer often requires hedges. Another common feature of the answers to a complex or subjective question are qualifying clauses, which are groups of words that subtly modify the meaning of the sentence. If the question or answer choice describes a rule to which there are exceptions or the subject matter is complicated, ambiguous, or confusing, the correct answer will require many words in order to be expressed clearly and accurately. In essence, you should not be deterred by answer choices that seem excessively long. Oftentimes, the author of the text will not be able to write the correct answer without

offering some qualifications and modifications. Your job is to read the answer choices thoroughly and completely and to select the one that most accurately and precisely answers the question.

13. Restating to Understand

Sometimes, a question on a multiple-choice test is difficult not because of what it asks but because of how it is written. If this is the case, restate the question or answer choice in different words. This process serves a couple of important purposes. First, it forces you to concentrate on the core of the question. In order to rephrase the question accurately, you have to understand it well. Rephrasing the question will concentrate your mind on the key words and ideas. Second, it will present the information to your mind in a fresh way. This process may trigger your memory and render some useful scrap of information picked up while studying.

14. True Statements

Sometimes an answer choice will be true in itself, but it does not answer the question. This is one of the main reasons why it is essential to read the question carefully and completely before proceeding to the answer choices. Too often, test takers skip ahead to the answer choices and look for true statements. Having found one of these, they are content to select it without reference to the question above. Obviously, this provides an easy way for test makers to play tricks. The savvy test taker will always read the entire question before turning to the answer choices. Then, having settled on a correct answer choice, he or she will refer to the original question and ensure that the selected answer is relevant. The mistake of choosing a correct-but-irrelevant answer choice is especially common on questions related to specific pieces of objective knowledge. A prepared test taker will have a wealth of factual knowledge at his or her disposal, and should not be careless in its application.

15. No Patterns

One of the more dangerous ideas that circulates about multiple-choice tests is that the correct answers tend to fall into patterns. These erroneous ideas range from a belief that B and C are the most common right answers, to the idea that an unprepared test-taker should answer "A-B-A-C-A-D-A-B-A." It cannot be emphasized enough that pattern-seeking of this type is exactly the WRONG way to approach a multiple-choice test. To begin with, it is highly unlikely that the test maker will plot the correct answers according to some predetermined pattern. The questions are scrambled and delivered in a random order. Furthermore, even if the test maker was following a pattern in the assignation of correct answers, there is no reason why the test taker would know which pattern he or she was using. Any attempt to discern a pattern in the answer choices is a waste of time and a distraction from the real work of taking the test. A test taker would be much better served by extra preparation before the test than by reliance on a pattern in the answers.

FREE DVD OFFER

Don't forget that doing well on your exam includes both understanding the test content and understanding how to use what you know to do well on the test. We offer a completely FREE Test Taking Tips DVD that covers world class test taking tips that you can use to be even more successful when you are taking your test.

All that we ask is that you email us your feedback about your study guide. To get your **FREE Test Taking Tips DVD**, email freedvd@studyguideteam.com with "FREE DVD" in the subject line and the following information in the body of the email:

- The title of your study guide.
- Your product rating on a scale of 1-5, with 5 being the highest rating.
- Your feedback about the study guide. What did you think of it?
- Your full name and shipping address to send your free DVD.

Introduction to the Praxis II English Language Arts: Content Knowledge (5038) Exam

Function of the Test

The Praxis II Elementary Education Content Knowledge (5038) exam is one of the Educational Testing Service's (ETS's) Subject Assessment tests. The Subject Assessment tests are intended to measure knowledge of more than ninety specific subjects taught by educators in kindergarten through twelfth grade classrooms, as well as teaching skills and knowledge in those subject areas. The tests are offered worldwide but are primarily used in the United States, where they are typically a required part of the certification and licensing procedure in certain states. They are also used as part of the licensing process by some professional associations and organizations.

The English Language Arts: Content Knowledge exam is designed to evaluate the knowledge, skills, and abilities of prospective secondary school English Language Arts teachers for teaching reading, language use, and communication. Individuals taking the test are usually enrolled in an English Language Arts education undergraduate degree program, have a degree already and are seeking an additional endorsement, or have recently moved to a state where the test is required or preferred.

Test Administration

The test is administered by computer through an international network of testing centers, including Prometric testing centers, some colleges and universities, as well as a variety of other locations. Although it is primarily used in the United States, the test is available at locations throughout the world. However, the test is not available at all times. Instead, there is a window of approximately two weeks per month during which the test may be taken. Test takers should be prepared to show proper identification at the testing center. Test takers will also receive an orientation to the computer testing procedure upon admission to the test center.

Accommodations for test takers meeting the requirements of the Americans with Disabilities Act include extended testing time, additional rest breaks, a separate testing room, a writer/recorder of answers, a test reader, and tests in sign language, Braille, audio, or large print. After twenty-one days from the initial exam attempt have elapsed, test takers may opt to retake the test at any time.

Test Format

The test is administered via computer, and all questions are selected response, in which the test taker chooses a particular word, sentence, or part of a graphic in a multiple-choice format, and numeric entry questions, in which the test taker gives a numeric answer. In both cases, the test taker receives a question from the computer and is prompted to select a response from the options on the screen. Questions may be answered in any order, and test takers may mark questions and return to them later.

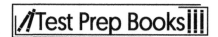

The exam contains content in three main categories, Reading, Language Use and Vocabulary, and Writing, Speaking, and Listening. The content of the exam is broken down as follows:

Subject	Questions	Percentage of Test
Reading	49	38%
Language Use and Vocabulary	33	25%
Writing, Speaking, and Listening	48	37%
Total	130	100%

Scoring

Raw scores are based on the number of correct responses; test takers are not penalized for incorrect answers or guesses. Each correct answer is worth one raw point. The raw scores are then converted to scaled scores that range from 100 to 200. The scaling process is intended to ensure that scores obtained by test takers who receive different versions of the test are comparable to each other. The required passing scaled score varies from state to state, from a low of 147 to a high of 167, with most states requiring at least a 167. The median score in 2015 was a 178.

ETS also offers a "Recognition of Excellence" to test takers who perform exceptionally well on the exam. The award is typically given to test takers whose scores fall in the top fifteen percent of scores on the exam.

Reading

Literature

Literature refers to a collection of written works that are the distinctive voices of peoples, time periods, and cultures. The world has gained great insight into human thought, vices, virtues, and desires through the written word. As the work pertains to the author's approach to these insights, literature can be classified as fiction or non-fiction.

Identifying Major Literary Works and Authors

The Praxis test assumes test takers will have a familiarity with a wide range of American, British, World, and Young Adult literary works. In most cases, the test taker will be presented with a quoted literary passage and be required to answer one or more questions about it. This may involve having to identify the literary work presented from a list of options.

The ability of the test taker to demonstrate familiarity of major literary works is key in success when taking Praxis exams. The following chart offers some examples of major works in addition to those listed elsewhere in this guide, but the list not exhaustive.

<u>American</u>
Fictional Prose
- Harriet Beecher Stowe | *Uncle Tom's Cabin*
- Ernest Hemingway | *For Whom the Bell Tolls*
- Jack London | *The Call of the Wild*
- Toni Morrison | *Beloved*
- N. Scott Momaday | *The Way to Rainy Mountain*
- J.D. Salinger | *Catcher in the Rye*
- John Steinbeck | *Grapes of Wrath*
- Alice Walker | *The Color Purple*

Drama
- Edward Albee | *Who's Afraid of Virginia Woolf?*
- Lorraine Hansberry | *A Raisin in the Sun*
- Amiri Baraka | *Dutchman*
- Eugene O'Neill |*Long Day's Journey into Night*
- Sam Shephard | *Buried Child*
- Thornton Wilder I *Our Town*
- Tennessee Williams | *A Streetcar Named Desire*

Poetry
- Anne Bradstreet | "In Reference to her Children, 23 June 1659"
- Emily Dickinson | "Because I could not stop for Death"
- Sylvia Plath | "Mirror"
- Langston Hughes | "Harlem"
- Edgar Allen Poe | "The Raven"

- Phillis Wheatley | "On Being Brought from Africa to America"
- Walt Whitman | "Song of Myself"

Literary Non-fiction
- Maya Angelou | *I Know Why the Caged Bird Sings*
- Truman Capote | In Cold Blood
- Frederick Douglass | *My Bondage and My Freedom*
- Archie Fire Lame Deer | The Gift of Power: The Life and Teachings of a Lakota Medicine Man
- Helen Keller | *The Story of My Life*
- Dave Pelzer | *A Child Called "It"*

British
Fictional Prose
- John Bunyan | *The Pilgrim's Progress*
- Joseph Conrad | *Heart of Darkness*
- Charles Dickens | *Tale of Two Cities*
- George Eliot | *Middlemarch*
- George Orwell | *1984*
- Mary Shelley | *Frankenstein*

Drama
- Samuel Beckett | *Waiting for Godot*
- Caryl Churchill | *Top Girls*
- William Congreve | *The Way of the World*
- Michael Frayn | *Noises Off*
- William Shakespeare | *Macbeth*
- Oscar Wilde | *The Importance of Being Earnest*

Poetry
- Elizabeth Barrett Browning | "How Do I Love Thee? (Sonnet 43)"
- Robert Burns | "A Red, Red Rose"
- Samuel Taylor Coleridge | "Rime of the Ancient Mariner"
- T.S. Eliot | "Love Song of J. Alfred Prufrock"
- John Milton | "Paradise Lost"

Literary Non-fiction
- Vera Brittain | *Testament of Youth*
- T. E. Lawrence | *Seven Pillars of Wisdom*
- Doris Lessing | *Going Home*
- Brian Blessed | *Absolute Pandemonium: The Autobiography*
- Virginia Woolf | *A Room of One's Own*

World
Fictional Prose
- Anonymous | *The Epic of Gilgamesh*
- Chinua Achebe | *Things Fall Apart*

- Margaret Atwood | *The Handmaid's Tale*
- Pearl S. Buck | *The Good Earth*
- Miguel de Cervantes | *Don Quixote*
- Fyodor Dostoyevsky | *Crime and Punishment*
- Gabriel Garcia Marquez | *One Hundred Years of Solitude*
- James Joyce | *Ulysses*
- Nikos Kazantzakis | *Zorba the Greek*
- Boris Pasternak | *Dr. Zhivago*
- Amy Tan | *The Joy Luck Club*
- Voltaire | *Candide*

Drama
- Bertolt Brecht | *Mother Courage and her Children*
- Anton Chekhov | *The Seagull*
- Lady Gregory | *Workhouse Ward*
- Henrik Ibsen | *A Doll's House*
- Luigi Pirandello | *Six Characters in Search of an Author*
- Molière | *Tartuffe*
- Sophocles | *Antigone*
- August Strindberg | *Miss Julie*
- Vyasa | *The Bhagavad Gita*
- Johann Wolfgang von Goethe | *Faust*

Poetry
- Anonymous | *Beowulf*
- Anonymous | *The Ramayana*
- Dante Alighieri | *The Divine Comedy*
- Federico García Lorca | *Gypsy Ballads*
- Omar Khayyám | *The Rubaiyat*
- Kahlil Gibran | *The Prophet*
- Andrew Barton "Banjo" Paterson | *"Waltzing Matilda"*
- Taslima Nasrin | *"Character"*
- Kostis Palamas | *"Ancient Eternal And Immortal Spirit"*
- Maria Elena Cruz Varela | *"Kaleidoscope"*
- King David | The 23rd Psalm, the Judeo-Christian Bible

Literary Non-fiction
- Pavel Basinsky | *Flight from Paradise*
- Jung Chang | *Wild Swans*
- Confucius | *The Analects of Confucius*
- Viktor Frankl | *Man's Search for Meaning*
- Mahatma Gandhi | *India of my Dreams*
- Nelson Mandela | *Long Walk to Freedom*
- Fatema Mernissi | *Beyond the Veil*
- Jonathan Swift | *"A Modest Proposal"*

<u>Young Adult</u>
Fictional Prose
- Jodi Lynn Anderson | *Tiger Lily*
- Lois Lowry | *The Giver*
- Scott O'Dell | *Island of the Blue Dolphins*
- Katherine Paterson Jacob | *Have I Loved*
- Antoine de Saint-Exupéry | *The Little Prince*
- Ellen Raskin | *The Westing Game*
- P. L. Travers | *Mary Poppins*
- Marcus Zusak | *The Book Thief*

Drama
- Peter Dee | *Voices from the High School*
- William Gibson | *The Miracle Worker*

Poetry
- Sandra Cisneros | "Eleven"
- Eamon Grennan | "Cat Scat"
- Tom Junod | "My Mother Couldn't Cook"
- Tupac Shakur | "The Rose that Grew from Concrete"

Literary Non-fiction
- Sherman Alexie | *The Absolutely True Diary of a Part-Time Indian*
- Anne Frank | *The Diary of Anne Frank*
- Philip Hoose | *The Boys who Challenged Hitler*
- Cynthia Levinson | *We've Got a Job*
- Malala Yousafzai and Christina Lamb | *I am Malala*

Identifying Literary Contexts

Understanding that works of literature emerged either because of a particular context—or perhaps despite a context—is key to analyzing them effectively.

<u>Historical Context</u>
The *historical context* of a piece of literature can refer to the time period, setting, or conditions of living at the time it was written as well as the context of the work. For example, Hawthorne's *The Scarlet Letter* was published in 1850, though the setting of the story is 1642-1649. Historically, then, when Hawthorne wrote his novel, the United States found itself at odds as the beginnings of a potential Civil War were in view. Thus, the historical context is potentially significant as it pertains to the ideas of traditions and values, which Hawthorne addresses in his story of Hester Prynne in the era of Puritanism.

<u>Cultural Context</u>
The *cultural context* of a piece of literature refers to cultural factors, such as the beliefs, religions, and customs that surround and are in a work of literature. The Puritan's beliefs, religion, and customs in Hawthorne's novel would be significant as they are at the core of the plot—the reason Hester wears the A and why Arthur kills himself. The customs of people in the Antebellum Period, though not quite as

restrictive, were still somewhat similar. This would impact how the audience of the time received the novel.

Literary Context

Literary context refers to the consideration of the genre, potentially at the time the work was written. In 1850, Realism and Romanticism were the driving forces in literature in the U.S., with depictions of life as it was at the time in which the work was written or the time it was written *about* as well as some works celebrating the beauty of nature. Thus, an audience in Hawthorne's time would have been well satisfied with the elements of both offered in the text. They would have been looking for details about everyday things and people (Realism), but they also would appreciate his approach to description of nature and the focus on the individual (American Romanticism). The contexts would be significant as they would pertain to evaluating the work against those criteria.

Here are some questions to use when considering context:

- When was the text written?
- What was society like at the time the text was written, or what was it like, given the work's identified time period?
- Who or what influenced the writer?
- What political or social influences might there have been?
- What influences may there have been in the genre that may have affected the writer?

Additionally, test takers should familiarize themselves with literary periods such as Old and Middle English, American Colonial, American Renaissance, American Naturalistic, and British and American Modernist and Post-Modernist movements. Most students of literature will have had extensive exposure to these literary periods in history, and while it is not necessary to recognize every major literary work on sight and associate that work to its corresponding movement or cultural context, the test taker should be familiar enough with the historical and cultural significance of each test passage in order to be able to address test questions correctly.

The following brief description of some literary contexts and their associated literary examples follows. It is not an all-inclusive list. The test taker should read each description, then follow up with independent study to clarify each movement, its context, its most familiar authors, and their works.

Metaphysical Poetry

Metaphysical poetry is the descriptor applied to 17th century poets whose poetry emphasized the lyrical quality of their work. These works contain highly creative poetic conceits or metaphoric comparisons between two highly dissimilar things or ideas. Metaphysical poetry is characterized by highly prosaic language and complicated, often layered, metaphor.

Poems such as John Donne's "The Flea," Andrew Marvell's "To His Coy Mistress," George Herbert's "The Collar," Henry Vaughan's "The World," and Richard Crashaw's "A Song" are associated with this type of poetry.

British Romanticism

British Romanticism was a cultural and literary movement within Europe that developed at the end of the 18th century and extended into the 19th century. It occurred partly in response to aristocratic, political, and social norms and partly in response to the Industrial Revolution of the day. Characterized by intense emotion, major literary works of British Romanticism embrace the idea of aestheticism and the beauty of nature. Literary works exalted folk customs and historical art and encouraged spontaneity of artistic endeavor. The movement embraced the heroic ideal and the concept that heroes would raise the quality of society.

Authors who are classified as British Romantics include Samuel Taylor Coleridge, John Keats, George Byron, Mary Shelley, Percy Bysshe Shelley, and William Blake. Well-known works include Samuel Taylor Coleridge's "Kubla Khan," John Keats' "Ode on a Grecian Urn," George Byron's "Childe Harold's Pilgrimage," Mary Shelley's *Frankenstein*, Percy Bysshe Shelley's "Ode to the West Wind," and William Blake's "The Tyger."

American Romanticism

American Romanticism occurred within the American literary scene beginning early in the 19th century. While many aspects were similar to British Romanticism, it is further characterized as having gothic aspects and the idea that individualism was to be encouraged. It also embraced the concept of the *noble savage*—the idea that indigenous culture uncorrupted by civilization is better than advanced society.

Well-known authors and works include Nathanial Hawthorne's *The House of the Seven Gables*, Edgar Allan Poe's "The Raven" and "The Cask of Amontillado," Emily Dickinson's "I Felt a Funeral in My Brain" and James Fenimore Cooper's *The Last of the Mohicans*.

Transcendentalism

Transcendentalism was a movement that applied to a way of thinking that developed within the United States, specifically New England, around 1836. While this way of thinking originally employed philosophical aspects, transcendentalism spread to all forms of art, literature, and even to the ways people chose to live. It was born out of a reaction to traditional rationalism and purported concepts such as a higher divinity, feminism, humanitarianism, and communal living. Transcendentalism valued intuition, self-reliance, and the idea that human nature was inherently good.

Well-known authors include Ralph Waldo Emerson, Henry David Thoreau, Louisa May Alcott, and Ellen Sturgis Hooper. Works include Ralph Waldo Emerson's "Self-Reliance" and "Uriel," Henry David Thoreau's *Walden* and *Civil Disobedience*, Louisa May Alcott's *Little Women*, and Ellen Sturgis Hooper's "I Slept, and Dreamed that Life was Beauty."

The Harlem Renaissance

The Harlem Renaissance is the descriptor given to the cultural, artistic, and social boom that developed in Harlem, New York, at the beginning of the 20th century, spanning the 1920s and 1930s. Originally termed *The New Negro Movement*, it emphasized African-American urban cultural expression and migration across the United States. It had strong roots in African-American Christianity, discourse, and intellectualism. The Harlem Renaissance heavily influenced the development of music and fashion as well. Its singular characteristic was to embrace Pan-American culturalisms; however, strong themes of the slavery experience and African-American folk traditions also emerged. A hallmark of the Harlem Renaissance was that it laid the foundation for the future Civil Rights Movement in the United States.

Well-known authors and works include Zora Neale Hurston's *Their Eyes Were Watching God*, Richard Wright's *Native Son*, Langston Hughes' "I, Too," and James Weldon Johnson's "God's Trombones: Seven Negro Sermons in Verse" and *The Book of American Negro Poetry*.

Understanding the Characteristics of Literary Genres

Classifying literature involves an understanding of the concept of genre. A *genre* is a category of literature that possesses similarities in style and in characteristics. Based on form and structure, there are four basic genres.

Fictional Prose

Fictional prose consists of fictional works written in standard form with a natural flow of speech and without poetic structure. Fictional prose primarily utilizes grammatically complete sentences and a paragraph structure to convey its message.

Drama

Drama is fiction that is written to be performed in a variety of media, intended to be performed for an audience, and structured for that purpose. It might be composed using poetry or prose, often straddling the elements of both in what actors are expected to present. Action and dialogue are the tools used in drama to tell the story.

Poetry

Poetry is fiction in verse that has a unique focus on the rhythm of language and focuses on intensity of feeling. It is not an entire story, though it may tell one; it is compact in form and in function. Poetry can be considered as a poet's brief word picture for a reader. Poetic structure is primarily composed of lines and stanzas. Together, poetic structure and devices are the methods that poets use to lead readers to feeling an effect and, ultimately, to the interpretive message.

Literary Nonfiction

Literary nonfiction is prose writing that is based on current or past real events or real people and includes straightforward accounts as well as those that offer opinions on facts or factual events. The Praxis exam distinguishes between *literary nonfiction*—a form of writing that incorporates literary styles and techniques to create factually-based narratives—and informational texts, which will be addressed in the next section.

Identifying Characteristics of Major Forms Within Each Genre

Fictional Prose

Fiction written in prose can be further broken down into **fiction genres**—types of fiction. Some of the more common genres of fiction are as follows:

- **Classical fiction**: a work of fiction considered timeless in its message or theme, remaining noteworthy and meaningful over decades or centuries—e.g., Charlotte Brontë's *Jane Eyre*, Mark Twain's *Adventures of Huckleberry Finn*

- **Fables**: short fiction that generally features animals, fantastic creatures, or other forces within nature that assume human-like characters and has a moral lesson for the reader—e.g., *Aesop's Fables*

- **Fairy tales**: children's stories with magical characters in imaginary, enchanted lands, usually depicting a struggle between good and evil, a sub-genre of folklore—e.g., Hans Christian Anderson's *The Little Mermaid*, *Cinderella* by the Brothers Grimm

- **Fantasy**: fiction with magic or supernatural elements that cannot occur in the real world, sometimes involving medieval elements in language, usually includes some form of sorcery or witchcraft and sometimes set on a different world—e.g., J.R.R. Tolkien's *The Hobbit*, J.K. Rowling's *Harry Potter and the Sorcerer's Stone*, George R.R. Martin's *A Game of Thrones*

- **Folklore**: types of fiction passed down from oral tradition, stories indigenous to a particular region or culture, with a local flavor in tone, designed to help humans cope with their condition in life and validate cultural traditions, beliefs, and customs—e.g., William Laughead's *Paul Bunyan and The Blue Ox*, the Buddhist story of "The Banyan Deer"

- **Mythology**: closely related to folklore but more widespread, features mystical, otherworldly characters and addresses the basic question of why and how humans exist, relies heavily on allegory and features gods or heroes captured in some sort of struggle—e.g., Greek myths, Genesis I and II in the Bible, Arthurian legends

- **Science fiction**: fiction that uses the principle of extrapolation—loosely defined as a form of prediction—to imagine future realities and problems of the human experience—e.g., Robert Heinlein's *Stranger in a Strange Land*, Ayn Rand's *Anthem*, Isaac Asimov's *I, Robot*, Philip K. Dick's *Do Androids Dream of Electric Sheep?*

- **Short stories**: short works of prose fiction with fully-developed themes and characters, focused on mood, generally developed with a single plot, with a short period of time for settings—e.g., Edgar Allan Poe's "Fall of the House of Usher," Shirley Jackson's "The Lottery," Isaac Bashevis Singer's "Gimpel the Fool"

Drama

Drama refers to a form of literature written for the purpose of performance for an audience. Like prose fiction, drama has several genres. The following are the most common ones:

- **Comedy**: a humorous play designed to amuse and entertain, often with an emphasis on the common person's experience, generally resolved in a positive way—e.g., Richard Sheridan's *School for Scandal*, Shakespeare's *Taming of the Shrew*, Neil Simon's *The Odd Couple*

- **History**: a play based on recorded history where the fate of a nation or kingdom is at the core of the conflict—e.g., Christopher Marlowe's *Edward II*, Shakespeare's *King Richard III*, Arthur Miller's *The Crucible*

- **Tragedy**: a serious play that often involves the downfall of the protagonist. In modern tragedies, the protagonist is not necessarily in a position of power or authority—e.g., Jean Racine's *Phèdre*, Arthur Miller's *Death of a Salesman*, John Steinbeck's *Of Mice and Men*

- **Melodrama**: a play that emphasizes heightened emotion and sensationalism, generally with stereotypical characters in exaggerated or realistic situations and with moral polarization—e.g., Jean-Jacques Rousseau's *Pygmalion*

- **Tragi-comedy**: a play that has elements of both tragedy—a character experiencing a tragic loss—and comedy—the resolution is often positive with no clear distinctive mood for either—e.g., Shakespeare's *The Merchant of Venice*, Anton Chekhov's *The Cherry Orchard*

Poetry

The genre of **poetry** refers to literary works that focus on the expression of feelings and ideas through the use of structure and linguistic rhythm to create a desired effect.

Different poetic structures and devices are used to create the various major forms of poetry. Some of the most common forms are discussed in the following chart.

Type	Poetic Structure	Example
Ballad	A poem or song passed down orally which tells a story and in English tradition usually uses an ABAB or ABCB rhyme scheme	William Butler Yeats' "The Ballad of Father O'Hart"
Epic	A long poem from ancient oral tradition which narrates the story of a legendary or heroic protagonist	Homer's *The Odyssey* Virgil's *The Aeneid*
Haiku	A Japanese poem of three unrhymed lines with five, seven, and five syllables (in English) with nature as a common subject matter	Matsuo Bashō "An old silent pond . . . A frog jumps into the pond, splash! Silence again."
Limerick	A five-line poem written in an AABBA rhyme scheme, with a witty focus	From Edward Lear's *Book of Nonsense*: "There was a Young Person of Smyrna Whose grandmother threatened to burn her . . ."
Ode	A formal lyric poem that addresses and praises a person, place, thing, or idea	Edna St. Vincent Millay's "Ode to Silence"
Sonnet	A fourteen-line poem written in iambic pentameter	Shakespeare's Sonnets 18 and 130

Literary nonfiction

Nonfiction works are best characterized by their subject matter, which must be factual and real, describing true life experiences. There are several common types of literary non-fiction.

Biography

A *biography* is a work written about a real person (historical or currently living). It involves factual accounts of the person's life, often in a re-telling of those events based on available, researched factual information. The re-telling and dialogue, especially if related within quotes, must be accurate and reflect reliable sources. A biography reflects the time and place in which the person lived, with the goal of creating an understanding of the person and his/her human experience. Examples of well-known biographies include *The Life of Samuel Johnson* by James Boswell and *Steve Jobs* by Walter Isaacson.

Autobiography

An *autobiography* is a factual account of a person's life written by that person. It may contain some or all of the same elements as a biography, but the author is the subject matter. An autobiography will be told in first person narrative. Examples of well-known autobiographies in literature include *Night* by Elie Wiesel and *Margaret Thatcher: The Autobiography* by Margaret Thatcher.

Memoir

A *memoir* is a historical account of a person's life and experiences written by one who has personal, intimate knowledge of the information. The line between memoir, autobiography, and biography is often muddled, but generally speaking, a memoir covers a specific timeline of events as opposed to the other forms of nonfiction. A memoir is less all-encompassing. It is also less formal in tone and tends to focus on the emotional aspect of the presented timeline of events. Some examples of memoirs in literature include *Angela's Ashes* by Frank McCourt and *All Creatures Great and Small* by James Herriot.

Journalism

Some forms of *journalism* can fall into the category of literary non-fiction—e.g., travel writing, nature writing, sports writing, the interview, and sometimes, the essay. Some examples include Elizabeth Kolbert's "The Lost World, in the Annals of Extinction series for *The New Yorker* and Gary Smith's "Ali and His Entourage" for *Sports Illustrated*.

Understanding Literary Interpretation

Literary interpretation is an interpretation and analysis of a literary work, based on the textual evidence in the work. It is often subjective as critical readers may discern different meanings in the details. A Praxis test taker needs to be prepared for questions that will test how well he or she can read a passage, make an analysis, and then provide evidence to support that analysis.

Literal and Figurative Meanings

When analyzing and interpreting fiction, readers must be active participants in the experience. Some authors make their messages clearer than others, but the onus is on the reader to add layers to what is read through interpretation. In literary interpretation, the goal is not to offer an opinion as to the inherent value of the work. Rather, the goal is to determine what the text means by analyzing the *literal and figurative meanings* of the text through critical reading.

Critical reading is close reading that elicits questions as the reader progresses. Many authors of fiction use literary elements and devices to further theme and to speak to their audience. These elements often utilize language that has an alternate or figurative meaning in addition to their actual or literal meaning. Readers should be asking questions about these and other important details as a passage is analyzed. What unfamiliar words are there? What is their contextual definition? How do they contribute to the overall feel of the work? How do they contribute to the mood and general message? Literal and figurative meanings are discussed further in the informational texts and rhetoric section.

Drawing Inferences

An *inference* refers to a point that is implied (as opposed to directly-stated) by the evidence presented. It's necessary to use inference in order to draw conclusions about the meaning of a passage. Authors make implications through character dialogue, thoughts, effects on others, actions, and looks.

When making an inference about a passage, it's important to rely only on the information that is provided in the text itself. This helps readers ensure that their conclusions are valid. Drawing inferences is also discussed in the informational texts and rhetoric section.

Textual Evidence

It's helpful to read a passage a few times, noting details that seem important to the piece. Textual evidence within the details helps readers draw a conclusion about a passage. *Textual evidence* refers to information—facts and examples that support the main idea. Textual evidence will likely come from

outside sources and can be in the form of quoted or paraphrased material. In order to draw a conclusion from evidence, it's important to examine the credibility and validity of that evidence as well as how (and if) it relates to the main idea. Effective use of textual evidence should connect to the main idea and support a specific point. Textual evidence is examined further in the informational texts and rhetoric section.

Understanding the Development of Themes

Identifying Theme or Central Message

The *theme* is the central message of a fictional work, whether that work is structured as prose, drama, or poetry. It is the heart of what an author is trying to say to readers through the writing, and theme is largely conveyed through literary elements and techniques.

In literature, a theme can often be determined by considering the over-arching narrative conflict within the work. Though there are several types of conflicts and several potential themes within them, the following are the most common:

- *Individual against the self*—relevant to themes of self-awareness, internal struggles, pride, coming of age, facing reality, fate, free will, vanity, loss of innocence, loneliness, isolation, fulfillment, failure, and disillusionment

- *Individual against nature*— relevant to themes of knowledge vs. ignorance, nature as beauty, quest for discovery, self-preservation, chaos and order, circle of life, death, and destruction of beauty

- *Individual against society*— relevant to themes of power, beauty, good, evil, war, class struggle, totalitarianism, role of men/women, wealth, corruption, change vs. tradition, capitalism, destruction, heroism, injustice, and racism

- *Individual against another individual*— relevant to themes of hope, loss of love or hope, sacrifice, power, revenge, betrayal, and honor

For example, in Hawthorne's *The Scarlet Letter*, one possible narrative conflict could be the individual against the self, with a relevant theme of internal struggles. This theme is alluded to through characterization—Dimmesdale's moral struggle with his love for Hester and Hester's internal struggles with the truth and her daughter, Pearl. It's also alluded to through plot—Dimmesdale's suicide and Hester helping the very townspeople who initially condemned her.

Sometimes, a text can convey a *message* or *universal lesson*—a truth or insight that the reader infers from the text, based on analysis of the literary and/or poetic elements. This message is often presented as a statement. For example, a potential message in Shakespeare's *Hamlet* could be "Revenge is what ultimately drives the human soul." This message can be immediately determined through plot and characterization in numerous ways, but it can also be determined through the setting of Norway, which is bordering on war.

How Authors Develop Theme

Authors employ a variety of techniques to present a theme. They may compare or contrast characters, events, places, ideas, or historical or invented settings to speak thematically. They may use analogies, metaphors, similes, allusions, or other literary devices to convey the theme. An author's use of diction, syntax, and tone can also help convey the theme. Authors will often develop themes through the development of characters, use of the setting, repetition of ideas, use of symbols, and through contrasting value systems. Authors of both fiction and nonfiction genres will use a variety of these techniques to develop one or more themes.

Regardless of the literary genre, there are commonalities in how authors, playwrights, and poets develop themes or central ideas.

Authors often do research, the results of which contributes to theme. In prose fiction and drama, this research may include real historical information about the setting the author has chosen or include elements that make fictional characters, settings, and plots seem realistic to the reader. In nonfiction, research is critical since the information contained within this literature must be accurate and, moreover, accurately represented.

In fiction, authors present a narrative conflict that will contribute to the overall theme. In fiction, this conflict may involve the storyline itself and some trouble within characters that needs resolution. In nonfiction, this conflict may be an explanation or commentary on factual people and events.

Authors will sometimes use character motivation to convey theme, such as in the example from *Hamlet* regarding revenge. In fiction, the characters an author creates will think, speak, and act in ways that effectively convey the theme to readers. In nonfiction, the characters are factual, as in a biography, but authors pay particular attention to presenting those motivations to make them clear to readers.

Authors also use literary devices as a means of conveying theme. For example, the use of moon symbolism in Mary Shelley's *Frankenstein* is significant as its phases can be compared to the phases that the Creature undergoes as he struggles with his identity.

The selected point of view can also contribute to a work's theme. The use of first-person point of view in a fiction or non-fiction work engages the reader's response differently than third person point of view. The central idea or theme from a first-person narrative may differ from a third-person limited text.

In literary nonfiction, authors usually identify the purpose of their writing, which differs from fiction, where the general purpose is to entertain. The purpose of nonfiction is usually to inform, persuade, or entertain the audience. The stated purpose of a non-fiction text will drive how the central message or theme, if applicable, is presented.

Authors identify an audience for their writing, which is critical in shaping the theme of the work. For example, the audience for J.K. Rowling's *Harry Potter* series would be different than the audience for a biography of George Washington. The audience an author chooses to address is closely tied to the purpose of the work. The choice of an audience also drives the choice of language and level of diction an author uses. Ultimately, the intended audience determines the level to which that subject matter is presented and the complexity of the theme.

Recognizing Universal Themes
Regardless of culture, place, or time, certain themes are universal to the human condition. Because all humans experience certain feelings and engage in similar experiences—birth, death, marriage, friendship, finding meaning, etc.—certain themes span cultures. However, different cultures have different norms and general beliefs concerning these themes. For example, the theme of maturing and crossing from childhood to adulthood is a global theme; however, the literature from one culture might imply that this happens in someone's twenties, while another culture's literature might imply that it happens in the early teenage years.

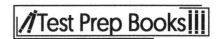

Identifying Literary Elements

There is no one, final definition of what literary elements are. They can be considered features or characteristics of fiction, but they are really more of a way that readers can unpack a text for the purpose of analysis and understanding the meaning. The elements contribute to a reader's literary interpretation of a passage as to how they function to convey the central message of a work. The most common literary elements used for analysis are the presented below.

Point of View
The *point of view* is the position the narrator takes when telling the story in prose. If a narrator is incorporated in a drama, the point of view may vary; in poetry, point of view refers to the position the speaker in a poem takes.

First Person
The first person point of view is when the writer uses the word "I" in the text. Poetry often uses first person, e.g., William Wordsworth's "I Wandered Lonely as a Cloud." Two examples of prose written in first person are Suzanne Collins' *The Hunger Games* and Anthony Burgess's *A Clockwork Orange*.

Second Person
The second person point of view is when the writer uses the pronoun "you." It is not widely used in prose fiction, but as a technique, it has been used by writers such as William Faulkner in *Absalom, Absalom!* and Albert Camus in *The Fall*. It is more common in poetry—e.g., Pablo Neruda's "If You Forget Me."

Third Person
Third person point of view is when the writer utilizes pronouns such as him, her, or them. It may be the most utilized point of view in prose as it provides flexibility to an author and is the one with which readers are most familiar. There are two main types of third person used in fiction. *Third person omniscient* uses a narrator that is all-knowing, relating the story by conveying and interpreting thoughts/feelings of all characters. In *third person limited,* the narrator relates the story through the perspective of one character's thoughts/feelings, usually the main character.

Plot
The *plot* is what happens in the story. Plots may be singular, containing one problem, or they may be very complex, with many sub-plots. All plots have exposition, a conflict, a climax, and a resolution. The *conflict* drives the plot and is something that the reader expects to be resolved. The plot carries those events along until there is a resolution to the conflict.

Tone
The *tone* of a story reflects the author's attitude and opinion about the subject matter of the story or text. Tone can be expressed through word choice, imagery, figurative language, syntax, and other details. The emotion or mood the reader experiences relates back to the tone of the story. Some examples of possible tones are humorous, somber, sentimental, and ironic.

Setting
The *setting* is the time, place, or set of surroundings in which the story occurs. It includes time or time span, place(s), climates, geography—man-made or natural—or cultural environments. Emily Dickinson's poem "Because I could not stop for Death" has a simple setting—the narrator's symbolic ride with Death

through town towards the local graveyard. Conversely, Leo Tolstoy's *War and Peace* encompasses numerous settings within settings in the areas affected by the Napoleonic Wars, spanning 1805 to 1812.

Dialogue and Story Events

Dialogue refers to the conversations that occur within a story. Dialogue can help to move the plot along and also to give insight into characters, setting, mood, and other aspects of the story. *Story events* are the different elements of a story that are ordered to create the plot.

Characters

Characters are the story's figures that assume primary, secondary, or minor roles. *Central* or *major* characters are those integral to the story—the plot cannot be resolved without them. A central character can be a *protagonist* or hero. There may be more than one protagonist, and he/she doesn't always have to possess good characteristics. A character can also be an *antagonist*—the force against a protagonist.

Dynamic characters change over the course of the plot time. *Static* characters do not change. A *symbolic* character is one that represents an author's idea about society in general—e.g., Napoleon in Orwell's *Animal Farm*. *Stock* characters are those that appear across genres and embrace stereotypes—e.g., the cowboy of the Wild West or the blonde bombshell in a detective novel. A *flat* character is one that does not present a lot of complexity or depth, while a *rounded* character does. Sometimes, the *narrator* of a story or the *speaker* in a poem can be a character—e.g., Nick Carraway in F. Scott Fitzgerald's *The Great Gatsby* or the speaker in Robert Browning's "My Last Duchess." The narrator might also function as a character in prose, though not be part of the story—e.g., Charles Dickens' narrator of *A Christmas Carol*.

Understanding Figurative Language

Whereas literal language is the author's use of precise words, proper meanings, definitions, and phrases that mean exactly what they say, *figurative language* deviates from precise meaning and word definition—often in conjunction with other familiar words and phrases—to paint a picture for the reader. Figurative language is less explicit and more open to reader interpretation.

Some examples of figurative language are included in the following graphic.

	Definition	Example
Simile	Compares two things using "like" or "as"	Her hair was like gold.
Metaphor	Compares two things as if they are the same	He was a giant teddy bear.
Idiom	Using words with predictable meanings to create a phrase with a different meaning	The world is your oyster.
Alliteration	Repeating the same beginning sound or letter in a phrase for emphasis	The busy baby babbled.
Personification	Attributing human characteristics to an object or an animal	The house glowered menacingly with a dark smile.
Foreshadowing	Giving an indication that something is going to happen later in the story	I wasn't aware at the time, but I would come to regret those words.
Symbolism	Using symbols to represent ideas and provide a different meaning	The ring represented the bond between us.
Onomatopoeia	Using words that imitate sound	The tire went off with a bang and a crunch.
Imagery	Appealing to the senses by using descriptive language	The sky was painted with red and pink and streaked with orange.
Hyperbole	Using exaggeration not meant to be taken literally	The girl weighed less than a feather.

Figurative language can be used to give additional insight into the theme or message of a text by moving beyond the usual and literal meaning of words and phrases. It can also be used to appeal to the senses of readers and create a more in-depth story.

Understanding Poetic Devices and Structure

Poetic Devices

Rhyme is the poet's use of corresponding word sounds in order to create an effect. Most rhyme occurs at the ends of a poem's lines, which is how readers arrive at the *rhyme scheme*. Each line that has a corresponding rhyming sound is assigned a letter—A, B, C, and so on. When using a rhyme scheme, poets will often follow lettered patterns.

Robert Frost's *"The Road Not Taken"* uses the ABAAB rhyme scheme:

Two roads diverged in a yellow wood,	A
And sorry I could not travel both	B
And be one traveler, long I stood	A
And looked down one as far as I could	A
To where it bent in the undergrowth;	B

Another important poetic device is *rhythm*—metered patterns within poetry verses. When a poet develops rhythm through *meter*, he or she is using a combination of stressed and unstressed syllables to create a sound effect for the reader.

Rhythm is created by the use of *poetic feet*—individual rhythmic units made up of the combination of stressed and unstressed syllables. A line of poetry is made up of one or more poetic feet. There are five standard types in English poetry, as depicted in the chart below.

Foot Type	Rhythm	Pattern
Iamb	buh Buh	Unstressed/stressed
Trochee	Buh buh	Stressed/unstressed
Spondee	Buh Buh	Stressed/stressed
Anapest	buh buh Buh	Unstressed/unstressed/stressed
Dactyl	Buh buh buh	Stressed/unstressed/unstressed

Structure

Poetry is most easily recognized by its structure, which varies greatly. For example, a structure may be strict in the number of lines it uses. It may use rhyming patterns or may not rhyme at all. There are three main types of poetic structures:

- *Verse*—poetry with a consistent meter and rhyme scheme
- *Blank verse*—poetry with consistent meter but an inconsistent rhyme scheme
- *Free verse*—poetry with inconsistent meter or rhyme

Verse poetry is most often developed in the form of *stanzas*—groups of word lines. Stanzas can also be considered *verses*. The structure is usually formulaic and adheres to the protocols for the form. For example, the English *sonnet* form uses a structure of fourteen lines and a variety of different rhyming patterns. The English *ode* typically uses three ten-line stanzas and has a particular rhyming pattern.

Poets choose poetic structure based on the effect they want to create. Some structures—such as the ballad and haiku—developed out of cultural influences and common artistic practice in history, but in more modern poetry, authors choose their structure to best fit their intended effect.

Identifying Reading Strategies

A *reading strategy* is the way a reader interacts with text in order to understand its meaning. It is a skill set that a reader brings to the reading. It employs a reader's ability to use prior knowledge when

addressing literature and utilizes a set of methods in order to analyze text. A reading strategy is not simply tackling a text passage as it appears. It involves a more complex system of planning and thought during the reading experience. Current research indicates readers who utilize strategies and a variety of critical reading skills are better thinkers who glean more interpretive information from their reading. Consequently, they are more successful in their overall comprehension.

Pre-reading Strategies

Pre-reading strategies are important, yet often overlooked. Non-critical readers will often begin reading without taking the time to review factors that will help them understand the text. Skipping pre-reading strategies may result in a reader having to re-address a text passage more times than is necessary. Some pre-reading strategies include the following:

- Previewing the text for clues
- Skimming the text for content
- Scanning for unfamiliar words in context
- Formulating questions on sight
- Making predictions
- Recognizing needed prior knowledge

Before reading a text passage, a reader can enhance his or her ability to comprehend material by *previewing the text for clues*. This may mean making careful note of any titles, headings, graphics, notes, introductions, important summaries, and conclusions. It can involve a reader making physical notes regarding these elements or highlighting anything he or she thinks is important before reading. Often, a reader will be able to gain information just from these elements alone. Of course, close reading is required in order to fill in the details. A reader needs to be able to ask what he or she is reading about and what a passage is trying to say. The answers to these general questions can often be answered in previewing the text itself.

It's helpful to use pre-reading clues to determine the main idea and organization. First, any titles, sub-headings, chapter headings should be read, and the test taker should make note of the author's credentials if any are listed. It's important to deduce what these clues may indicate as it pertains to the focus of the text and how it's organized.

During pre-reading, readers should also take special note of how text features contribute to the central idea or thesis of the passage. Is there an index? Is there a glossary? What headings, footnotes, or other visuals are included and how do they relate to the details within the passage? Again, this is where any pre-reading notes come in handy, since a test taker should be able to relate supporting details to these textual features.

Next, a reader should *skim* the text for general ideas and content. This technique does not involve close reading; rather, it involves looking for important words within the passage itself. These words may have something to do with the author's theme. They may have to do with structure—for example, words such as *first, next, therefore*, and *last*. Skimming helps a reader understand the overall structure of a passage and, in turn, this helps him or her understand the author's theme or message.

From there, a reader should quickly *scan* the text for any unfamiliar words. When reading a print text, highlighting these words or making other marginal notation is helpful when going back to read text critically. A reader should look at the words surrounding any unfamiliar ones to see what contextual clues unfamiliar words carry. Being able to define unfamiliar terms through contextual meaning is a critical skill in reading comprehension.

A reader should also *formulate any questions* he or she might have before conducting close reading. Questions such as "What is the author trying to tell me?" or "Is the author trying to persuade my thinking?" are important to a reader's ability to engage critically with the text. Questions will focus a reader's attention on what is important in terms of idea and what is supporting detail.

Along with formulating questions, it is helpful to make predictions of what the answers to these questions and others will be. *Making predictions* involves using information from the text and personal experiences to make a thoughtful guess as to what will happen in the story and what outcomes can be expected.

Last, a reader should recognize that authors assume readers bring a prior knowledge set to the reading experience. Not all readers have the same experience, but authors seek to communicate with their readers. In turn, readers should strive to interact with the author of a particular passage by asking themselves what the passage demands they know during reading. This is also known as making a text-to-self connection. If a passage is informational in nature, a reader should ask "What do I know about this topic from other experiences I've had or other works I've read?" If a reader can relate to the content, he or she will better understand it.

All of the above pre-reading strategies will help the reader prepare for a closer reading experience. They will engage a reader in active interaction with the text by helping to focus the reader's full attention on the details that he or she will encounter during the next round or two of critical, closer reading.

Strategies During Reading

After pre-reading, a test taker can employ a variety of other reading strategies while conducting one or more closer readings. These strategies include the following:

- Clarifying during a close read
- Questioning during a close read
- Organizing the main ideas and supporting details
- Summarizing the text effectively

A reader needs to be able to *clarify* what he or she is reading. This strategy demands a reader think about how and what he or she is reading. This thinking should occur during and after the act of reading. For example, a reader may encounter one or more unfamiliar ideas during reading, then be asked to apply thoughts about those unfamiliar concepts after reading when answering test questions.

Questioning during a critical read is closely related to clarifying. A reader must be able to ask questions in general about what he or she is reading and questions regarding the author's supporting ideas. Questioning also involves a reader's ability to self-question. When closely reading a passage, it's not enough to simply try and understand the author. A reader must consider critical thinking questions to ensure he or she is comprehending intent. It's advisable, when conducting a close read, to write out margin notes and questions during the experience. These questions can be addressed later in the thinking process after reading and during the phase where a reader addresses the test questions. A reader who is successful in reading comprehension will iteratively question what he or she reads, search text for clarification, then answer any questions that arise.

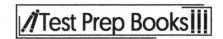

A reader should *organize* main ideas and supporting details cognitively as he or she reads, as it will help the reader understand the larger structure at work. The use of quick annotations or marks to indicate what the main idea is and how the details function to support it can be helpful. Understanding the structure of a text passage is sometimes critical to answering questions about an author's approach, theme, messages, and supporting detail. This strategy is most effective when reading informational or nonfiction text. Texts that try to convince readers of a particular idea, that present a theory, or that try to explain difficult concepts are easier to understand when a reader can identify the overarching structure at work.

Post-reading Strategies

After completing a text, a reader should be able to *summarize* the author's theme and supporting details in order to fully understand the passage. Being able to effectively restate the author's message, sub-themes, and pertinent, supporting ideas will help a reader gain an advantage when addressing standardized test questions.

A reader should also evaluate the strength of the predictions that were made in the pre-reading stage. Using textual evidence, predictions should be compared to the actual events in the story to see if the two were similar or not. Employing all of these strategies will lead to fuller, more insightful reading comprehension.

Demonstrating Common Research-Based Strategies for Reading Instruction

The Praxis tests will assess educational candidates' familiarity with common research-based strategies for reading instruction. This will require potential teachers to be knowledgeable in current practices as well as able to evaluate the effectiveness of those practices as applicable to reading tasks and apply them to reading instruction challenges.

As this is a widely varied topic across educational levels, student abilities, and many reading comprehension skills, the potential test taker is advised to read further on the subject. Many online resources are available, but some additional works to consider include:

- McGregor, Tanny. *Comprehension Connections: Bridges to Strategic Reading*. Portsmouth, New Hampshire: Heinemann, 2007.

- Miller, Brett, Cutting, Laurie E., McCardle, Peggy. *Unraveling Reading Comprehension*. Baltimore, Maryland: Paul H. Brooks Publishing Co., Inc. 2013.

- Tovani, Cris. *I Read it, but I Don't Get it: Comprehension Strategies for Adolescent Readers*. Portland, ME: Stenhouse Publishing, 2000.

- Wilhelm, Jeffrey D. *Improving Comprehension with Think-Aloud Strategies*. New York, New York: Scholastic Inc., 2001.

A potential educator needs to be aware that teaching reading comprehension involves developing skills beyond mere word recognition. It involves being able to teach critical thinking skills and being able to teach students how to process unfamiliar material based on prior knowledge. It involves getting students involved in what they read, based on their interests, and their ability to relate to the material. It involves encouraging students to ask questions and explore.

In demonstrating one's ability to use common research-based strategies for reading instruction, a potential test taker should be able to show his or her awareness of theory regarding how to activate students' prior knowledge, how to model meta-cognitive practices, and how to employ multiple reading strategies for a variety of situations for the most comprehensive student experience.

Activating Prior Knowledge

Activating students' prior knowledge—sometimes referred to as *schemas*—means being able to get students to ascertain what they already know, so they can apply it to their reading. A common strategy to use prior to reading is a K-W-L chart, a graphic organizer which has students determine what they already know about a topic, what they want to know, and what they learned after reading. Having students complete the K section before reading is a tangible way to activate their schemas.

It is important students make connections and relate reading passages to their own experiences— referred to as *text to self*, to their world knowledge— referred to as *text to world*, and to other texts— referred to as *text to text*. The ability to make these connections helps students better understand what they have read.

Potential teachers should be able to model asking questions during the reading experience and model the finding of those answers, based on prior knowledge. Having students read, then write about the connections they make to the text will increase reading comprehension skills. Of course, teaching students to activate and use their schema as it applies to their reading is a skill that should be taught over time. Encourage students to ask how text passages relate to what they already know within their own lives, how those passages relate to what they already know about the world, and how those passages relate to other things they've read. Doing so will result in more critical thinkers and, in turn, more critical readers.

Metacognitive Practices

Metacognitive strategies ask the student to decode text passages. In part, they require the student to preview text, be able to recognize unfamiliar words, then use context clues to define them for greater understanding. In addition, meta-cognitive strategies in the classroom employ skills such as being able to decode imagery, being able to predict, and being able to summarize. If a student can define unfamiliar vocabulary, make sense of an author's use of imagery, preview text prior to reading, predict outcomes during reading, and summarize the material, he or she is achieving effective reading comprehension. When approaching reading instruction, the teacher who encourages students to use phrases such as *I'm noticing*, *I'm thinking*, and *I'm wondering* is teaching a meta-cognitive type strategy.

Active Reading

It has been shown that the teacher who employs multiple reading strategies in a variety of reading situations has the most success in fostering critical thinkers. Teachers should strive to make reading an active, observable process. *Active reading* involves reading with a purpose and determination to not only understand, but evaluate text using critical reading skills. Critical reading skills need to be fostered in a way that allows students to read and retain information and then gain interactive feedback experience with peers and with an instructor. Employing multiple reading strategies, either through assigned, independent reading with follow up or through a shared experience, aids in active reading.

The following are some of the reading strategies that should be utilized:

- Modeling prediction
- Modeling inference
- Asking students to connect text to self, the world, and to other text
- Asking students to visualize what they read (playing the "video" in their head)
- Asking students to partner in their reading experiences
- Helping students determine the importance of ideas in what they read
- Modeling the critical thinking process
- Modeling analyzation
- Modeling summarization

Identifying Literary Theories

A *literary theory* can be considered a methodology for understanding literature. It asks, "What is literature?" and offers readers a working set of principles to understand common themes, ideas, and intent. Classifications of literary theory are often referred to as *schools of thought*. These schools are based on subdivisions in historical perspective and in philosophical thinking across literary analysts and critics.

Romanticism/Aestheticism

Romanticism/Aestheticism spanned the 19th century and developed in response to the idea that enlightenment and reason were the source of all truth and authority in philosophy. Romanticism and Aestheticism embraced the tenet that *aesthetics*—all that is beautiful and natural—in art and literature should be considered the highest-held principle, overriding all others. Popular authors include Oscar Wilde, Edgar Allan Poe, Mary Shelley, and John Keats.

Marxism

Marxism as a literary theory developed in the early twentieth century after the Russian October Revolution of 1917. It loosely embraced the idea that social realism was the highest form of literature and that the social classes' struggle for progress was the most important concept literature could emphasize. Examples of authors include Simone de Beauvoir and Bertolt Brecht.

Structuralism

Structuralism included all aspects of philosophy, linguistics, anthropology, and literary theory. Beginning in the early 1900s, this school of thought focused on ideas surrounding how human culture is understood within its larger structures and how those structures influence people's thoughts and actions. Specifically, structuralism examines how literature is interconnected through structure. It examines common elements in the stories and the myths that contribute to literature as a whole. Popular theorists and writers include Claude Levi-Strauss, Umberto Eco, and Roland Barthes.

Post-Structuralism and Deconstruction

Post-Structuralism and *deconstruction* developed out of structuralism in the twentieth century. It expanded on the idea of overall structure in literature, but both theories argue varying analytical concepts of how that structure should be examined and utilized. For example, while structuralism acknowledges oppositional relationships in literature—e.g., male/female, beginning/end, rational/emotional—post-structuralism and deconstruction began de-emphasizing the idea that one idea is always dominant over another. Both also assert that studying text also means studying the

knowledge that produced the text. Popular theorists and writers include Roland Barthes and Michel Foucault.

New Criticism

New Criticism dominated American culture in the mid-twentieth century. It purports that close, critical reading was necessary to understanding literary works, especially poetry. Popular theory also focused on the inherent beauty of text itself. New Criticism rejected the previous critical focus of how history, use of language, and the author's experience influence literature, asserting those ideas as being too loosely interpretive in examining literature. As a movement, it tended to separate literature from historical context and an author's intent. It embraced the idea that formal study of structure and text should not be separated. Theorists of note include Stephen Greenblatt and Jonathan Goldberg.

Informational Texts and Rhetoric

Informational texts are a category of texts within the genre of nonfiction. Their intent is to inform, and while they do convey a point of view and may include literary devices, they do not utilize other literary elements, such as characters or plot. An informational text also reflects a *thesis*—an implicit or explicit statement of the text's intent and/or a *main idea*—the overarching focus and/or purpose of the text, generally implied. Some examples of informational texts are informative articles, instructional/how-to texts, factual reports, reference texts, and self-help texts.

Interpreting Textual Evidence in Informational Text

Literal and Figurative Meanings

It is important when evaluating informational texts to consider the use of both *literal and figurative meanings*. The words and phrases an author chooses to include in a text must be evaluated. How does the word choice affect the meaning and tone? By recognizing the use of literal and figurative language, a reader can more readily ascertain the message or purpose of a text. Literal word choice is the easiest to analyze as it represents the usual and intended way a word or phrase is used. It is also more common in informational texts because it is used to state facts and definitions. While figurative language is typically associated with fiction and poetry, it can be found in informational texts as well. The reader must determine not only what is meant by the figurative language in context, but also how the author intended it to shape the overall text.

Inference in Informational Text

Inference refers to the reader's ability to understand the unwritten text, i.e., "read between the lines" in terms of an author's intent or message. The strategy asks that a reader not take everything he or she reads at face value but instead, add his or her own interpretation of what the author seems to be trying to convey. A reader's ability to make inferences relies on his or her ability to think clearly and logically about the text. It does not ask that the reader make wild speculation or guess about the material but demands that he or she be able to come to a sound conclusion about the material.

An author's use of less literal words and phrases requires readers to make more inference when they read. Since inference involves *deduction*—deriving conclusions from ideas assumed to be true—there's more room for interpretation. Still, critical readers who employ inference, if careful in their thinking, can still arrive at the logical, sound conclusions the author intends.

Textual Evidence in Informational Text

Once a reader has determined an author's thesis or main idea, he or she will need to understand how textual evidence supports interpretation of that thesis or main idea. Test takers will be asked direct questions regarding an author's main idea and may be asked to identify evidence that would support those ideas. This will require test takers to comprehend literal and figurative meanings within the text passage, be able to draw inferences from provided information, and be able to separate important evidence from minor supporting detail. It's often helpful to skim test questions and answer options prior to critically reading informational text; however, test takers should avoid the temptation to solely look for the correct answers. Just trying to find the "right answer" may cause test takers to miss important supporting textual evidence. Making mental note of test questions is only helpful as a guide when reading.

After identifying an author's thesis or main idea, a test taker should look at the supporting details that the author provides to back up his or her assertions, identifying those additional pieces of information that help expand the thesis. From there, test takers should examine the additional information and related details for credibility, the author's use of outside sources, and be able to point to direct evidence that supports the author's claims. It's also imperative that test takers be able to identify what is strong support and what is merely additional information that is nice to know but not necessary. Being able to make this differentiation will help test takers effectively answer questions regarding an author's use of supporting evidence within informational text.

Understanding Organizational Patterns and Structures

Informational text is specifically designed to relate factual information, and although it is open to a reader's interpretation and application of the facts, the structure of the presentation is carefully designed to lead the reader to a particular conclusion or central idea. When reading informational text, it is important that readers are able to understand its organizational structure as the structure often directly relates to an author's intent to inform and/or persuade the reader.

Central Idea

The first step in identifying the text's structure is to determine the thesis or main idea. The thesis statement and organization of a work are closely intertwined. *A thesis statement* indicates the writer's purpose and may include the scope and direction of the text. It may be presented at the beginning of a text or at the end, and it may be explicit or implicit.

Organizational Pattern

Once a reader has a grasp of the thesis or main idea of the text, he or she can better determine its organizational structure. Test takers are advised to read informational text passages more than once in order to comprehend the material fully. It is also helpful to examine any text features present in the text including the table of contents, index, glossary, headings, footnotes, and visuals. The analysis of these features and the information presented within them, can offer additional clues about the central idea and structure of a text.

The following questions should be asked when considering structure:

- How does the author assemble the parts to make an effective whole argument?
- Is the passage linear in nature and if so, what is the timeline or thread of logic?
- What is the presented order of events, facts, or arguments? Are these effective in contributing to the author's thesis?
- How can the passage be divided into sections? How are they related to each other and to the main idea or thesis?
- What key terms are used to indicate the organization?

Next, test takers should skim the passage, noting the first line or two of each body paragraph—the *topic sentences*—and the conclusion. Key *transitional terms*, such as *on the other hand*, *also*, *because*, *however*, *therefore*, *most importantly*, and *first*, within the text can also signal organizational structure. Based on these clues, readers should then be able to identify what type of organizational structure is being used. The following organizational structures are most common:

- *Problem/solution*—organized by an analysis/overview of a problem, followed by potential solution(s)

- *Cause/effect*—organized by the effects resulting from a cause or the cause(s) of a particular effect

- *Spatial order*—organized by points that suggest location or direction—e.g., top to bottom, right to left, outside to inside

- *Chronological/sequence order*—organized by points presented to indicate a passage of time or through purposeful steps/stages

- *Comparison/Contrast*—organized by points that indicate similarities and/or differences between two things or concepts

- *Order of importance*—organized by priority of points, often most significant to least significant or vice versa

Understanding the Effect of Word Choice

An author's choice of words—also referred to as *diction*—helps to convey his or her meaning in a particular way. Through diction, an author can convey a particular tone—e.g., a humorous tone, a serious tone—in order to support the thesis in a meaningful way to the reader.

Connotation and Denotation

Connotation is when an author chooses words or phrases that invoke ideas or feelings other than their literal meaning. An example of the use of connotation is the word *cheap*, which suggests something is poor in value or negatively describes a person as reluctant to spend money. When something or someone is described this way, the reader is more inclined to have a particular image or feeling about it or him/her. Thus, connotation can be a very effective language tool in creating emotion and swaying opinion. However, connotations are sometimes hard to pin down because varying emotions can be associated with a word. Generally, though, connotative meanings tend to be fairly consistent within a specific cultural group.

Denotation refers to words or phrases that mean exactly what they say. It is helpful when a writer wants to present hard facts or vocabulary terms with which readers may be unfamiliar. Some examples of denotation are the words *inexpensive* and *frugal*. *Inexpensive* refers to the cost of something, not its value, and *frugal* indicates that a person is conscientiously watching his or her spending. These terms do not elicit the same emotions that *cheap* does.

Authors sometimes choose to use both, but what they choose and when they use it is what critical readers need to differentiate. One method isn't inherently better than the other; however, one may create a better effect, depending upon an author's intent. If, for example, an author's purpose is to inform, to instruct, and to familiarize readers with a difficult subject, his or her use of connotation may be helpful. However, it may also undermine credibility and confuse readers. An author who wants to create a credible, scholarly effect in his or her text would most likely use denotation, which emphasizes literal, factual meaning and examples.

Technical Language

Test takers and critical readers alike should be very aware of technical language used within informational text. *Technical language* refers to terminology that is specific to a particular industry and is best understood by those specializing in that industry. This language is fairly easy to differentiate, since it will most likely be unfamiliar to readers. It's critical to be able to define technical language either by the author's written definition, through the use of an included glossary—if offered—or through context clues that help readers clarify word meaning.

Explicit and Inferred Text

Making an inference requires the reader to read between the lines and look for what is implied rather than what is directly stated. That is, using information that is known from the text, the reader is able to make a logical assumption about information that is not directly stated but is probably true.

Identifying Rhetorical Strategies

Rhetoric refers to an author's use of particular strategies, appeals, and devices to persuade an intended audience. The more effective the use of rhetoric, the more likely the audience will be persuaded.

Determining an Author's Point of View

A *rhetorical strategy*—also referred to as a *rhetorical mode*—is the structural way an author chooses to present his/her argument. Though the terms noted below are similar to the organizational structures noted earlier, these strategies do not imply that the entire text follows the approach. For example, a cause and effect organizational structure is solely that, nothing more. A persuasive text may use cause and effect as a strategy to convey a singular point. Thus, an argument may include several of the strategies as the author strives to convince his or her audience to take action or accept a different point of view. It's important that readers are able to identify an author's thesis and position on the topic in order to be able to identify the careful construction through which the author speaks to the reader. The following are some of the more common rhetorical strategies:

- *Cause and effect*—establishing a logical correlation or causation between two ideas
- *Classification/division*—the grouping of similar items together or division of something into parts
- *Comparison/contrast*—the distinguishing of similarities/differences to expand on an idea
- *Definition*—used to clarify abstract ideas, unfamiliar concepts, or to distinguish one idea from another
- *Description*—use of vivid imagery, active verbs, and clear adjectives to explain ideas
- *Exemplification*—the use of examples to explain an idea
- *Narration*—anecdotes or personal experience to present or expand on a concept
- *Problem/Solution*—presentation of a problem or problems, followed by proposed solution(s)

Rhetorical Strategies and Devices

A *rhetorical device* is the phrasing and presentation of an idea that reinforces and emphasizes a point in an argument. A rhetorical device is often quite memorable. One of the more famous uses of a rhetorical device is in John F. Kennedy's 1961 inaugural address: "Ask not what your country can do for you, ask what you can do for your country." The contrast of ideas presented in the phrasing is an example of the rhetorical device of antimetabole.

Some other common examples are provided below, but test takers should be aware that this is not a complete list.

Device	Definition	Example
Allusion	A reference to a famous person, event, or significant literary text as a form of significant comparison	"We are apt to shut our eyes against a painful truth, and listen to the song of that siren till she transforms us into beasts." Patrick Henry
Anaphora	The repetition of the same words at the beginning of successive words, phrases, or clauses, designed to emphasize an idea	"We shall not flag or fail. We shall go on to the end. We shall fight in France, we shall fight on the seas and oceans, we shall fight with growing confidence … we shall fight in the fields and in the streets, we shall fight in the hills. We shall never surrender." Winston Churchill
Understatement	A statement meant to portray a situation as less important than it actually is to create an ironic effect	"The war in the Pacific has not necessarily developed in Japan's favor." Emperor Hirohito, surrendering Japan in World War II
Parallelism	A syntactical similarity in a structure or series of structures used for impact of an idea, making it memorable	"A penny saved is a penny earned." Ben Franklin
Rhetorical question	A question posed that is not answered by the writer though there is a desired response, most often designed to emphasize a point	"Can anyone look at our reduced standing in the world today and say, 'Let's have four more years of this?'" Ronald Reagan

Understanding Methods Used to Appeal to a Specific Audience

Methods of Appeal or Persuasion

In an argument or persuasive text, an author will strive to sway readers to an opinion or conclusion. To be effective, an author must consider his or her intended audience. Although an author may write text for a general audience, he or she will use methods of appeal or persuasion to convince that audience. Aristotle asserted that there were three methods or modes by which a person could be persuaded. These are referred to as *rhetorical appeals*.

The three main types of rhetorical appeals are shown in the following graphic.

Ethos, also referred to as an *ethical appeal*, is an appeal to the audience's perception of the writer as credible (or not), based on their examination of their ethics and who the writer is, his/her experience or incorporation of relevant information, or his/her argument. For example, authors may present testimonials to bolster their arguments. The reader who critically examines the veracity of the testimonials and the credibility of those giving the testimony will be able to determine if the author's use of testimony is valid to his or her argument. In turn, this will help the reader determine if the author's thesis is valid. An author's careful and appropriate use of technical language can create an overall knowledgeable effect and, in turn, act as a convincing vehicle when it comes to credibility. Overuse of technical language, however, may create confusion in readers and obscure an author's overall intent.

Pathos, also referred to as a *pathetic* or *emotional appeal*, is an appeal to the audience's sense of identity, self-interest, or emotions. A critical reader will notice when the author is appealing to pathos through anecdotes and descriptions that elicit an emotion such as anger or pity. Readers should also beware of factual information that uses generalization to appeal to the emotions. While it's tempting to believe an author is the source of truth in his or her text, an author who presents factual information as universally true, consistent throughout time, and common to all groups is using *generalization*. Authors who exclusively use generalizations without specific facts and credible sourcing are attempting to sway readers solely through emotion.

Logos, also referred to as a *logical appeal*, is an appeal to the audience's ability to see and understand the logic in a claim offered by the writer. A critical reader has to be able to evaluate an author's arguments for validity of reasoning and for sufficiency when it comes to argument.

Understanding Development of a Written Argument

Evaluating an Author's Purpose

A reader must be able to evaluate the argument or point the author is trying to make and determine if it is adequately supported. The first step is to determine the main idea. The main idea is what the author wants to say about a specific topic. The next step is to locate the supporting details. An author uses supporting details to illustrate the main idea. These are the details that provide evidence or examples to help make a point. Supporting details often appear in the form of quotations, paraphrasing, or analysis. Test takers should then examine the text to make sure the author connects details and analysis to the main point. These steps are crucial to understanding the text and evaluating how well the author presents his or her argument and evidence. The following graphic demonstrates the connection between the main idea and the supporting details.

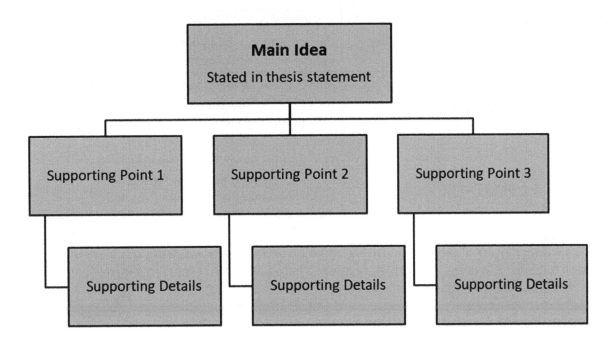

Evaluating Evidence

It is important to evaluate the author's supporting details to be sure that they are credible, provide evidence of the author's point, and directly support the main idea. Critical readers examine the facts used to support an author's argument and check those facts against other sources to be sure the facts are correct. They also check the validity of the sources used to be sure those sources are credible, academic, and/or peer-reviewed. A strong argument uses valid, measurable facts to support ideas.

Identifying False Statements

A reader must also be able to identify any *logical fallacies*—logically-flawed statements—that an author may make as those fallacies impact the validity and veracity of the author's claims.

Some of the more common fallacies are shown in the following chart.

Fallacy	Definition
Slippery Slope	A fallacy that is built on the idea that a particular action will lead to a series of events with negative results
Red Herring	The use of an observation or distraction to remove attention from the actual issue
Straw Man	An exaggeration or misrepresentation of an argument so that it is easier to refute
Post Hoc Ergo Propter Hoc	A fallacy that assumes an event to be the consequence of an earlier event merely because it came after it
Bandwagon	A fallacy that assumes because the majority of people feel or believe a certain way then it must be the right way
Ad Hominem	The use of a personal attack on the person or persons associated with a certain argument rather than focusing on the actual argument itself

Readers who are aware of the types of fallacious reasoning are able to weigh the credibility of the author's statements in terms of effective argument. Rhetorical text that contains a myriad of fallacious statements should be considered ineffectual and suspect.

Interpreting Media and Non-Print Text

This study guide has primarily focused on the printed word for Praxis test takers; however, it's important to note media and non-print text. In the 21st century, rhetoric is evident in a variety of formats. Blogs, vlogs, videos, news footage, advertisements, and live video fill informational feeds, and readers see many shortened images and snapshot texts a day. It's important to note that the majority of these formats use images to appeal to emotion over factual information. Online visuals spread more quickly and are more easily adopted by consumers as fact than printed formats.

Critical readers should be aware that media and non-print text carries some societal weight to the population. In being inundated with pictures and live footage, readers often feel compelled to skip the task of critical reading analysis and accept truth at literal face value. Authors of non-print media are aware of this fact and frequently capitalize on it.

To critically address non-print media requires that the consumer address additional sources and not exclude printed text in order to reach sound conclusions. While it's tempting for consumers to get swept away in the latest viral media, it's important to remember that creators of such have an agenda, and unless the non-print media in question is backed up with sound supporting evidence, any thesis or

message cannot be considered valid or factual. Memes, gifs, and looped video cannot tell the whole, truthful story although they may appeal to opinions with which readers already agree. Sharing such non-print media online can precipitate widespread misunderstanding.

When presented with non-print media, critical readers should consider these bits of information as teasers to be investigated for accuracy and veracity. Of course, certain non-print media exists solely for entertainment, but the critical reader should be able to separate out what's generalized for entertainment's sake and what's presented for further verification, before blindly accepting the message. Increasingly, this has become more difficult for readers to do, only because of the onslaught of information to which they are exposed.

If a reader is not to fall prey to strong imagery and non-print media, he or she will need to fact-check. This, of course, requires time and attention on the reader's part, and in current culture, taking the time to fact-check seems counterproductive. However, in order to maintain credibility themselves, readers must be able to evaluate multiple sources of information across media formats and be able to identify the emotional appeal used in the smaller sound bites of non-print media. Readers must view with a discerning eye, listen with a questioning ear, and think with a critical mind.

Practice Questions

1. Read the following poem. Which option best expresses the symbolic meaning of the "road" and the overall theme?

>Two roads diverged in a yellow wood,
>And sorry I could not travel both
>And be one traveler, long I stood
>And looked down one as far as I could
>To where it bent in the undergrowth;
>Then took the other, as just as fair,
>And having perhaps the better claim,
>Because it was grassy and wanted wear;
>Though as for that the passing there
>Had worn them really about the same,
>And both that morning equally lay
>In leaves no step had trodden black.
>Oh, I kept the first for another day!
>Yet knowing how way leads on to way,
>I doubted if I should ever come back.
>I shall be telling this with a sigh
>Somewhere ages and ages hence:
>Two roads diverged in a wood, and I—
>I took the one less traveled by,
>And that has made all the difference—Robert Frost, "The Road Not Taken"

   a. A divergent spot where the traveler had to choose the correct path to his destination
   b. A choice between good and evil that the traveler needs to make
   c. The traveler's struggle between his lost love and his future prospects
   d. Life's journey and the choices with which humans are faced

2. Which option best exemplifies an author's use of *alliteration* and *personification*?
   a. Her mood hung about her like a weary cape, very dull from wear.
   b. It shuddered, swayed, shook, and screamed its way into dust under hot flames.
   c. The house was a starch sentry, warning visitors away.
   d. At its shoreline, visitors swore they heard the siren call of the cliffs above.

3. Read the following poem. Which option best depicts the rhyme scheme?

>A slumber did my spirit seal;
>I had no human fears:
>She seemed a thing that could not feel
>The touch of earthly years.—from William Wordsworth, "A Slumber Did My Spirit Seal"

   a. BAC BAC
   b. ABAB
   c. ABBA
   d. AB CD AB

4. Read the following poem. Which option describes its corresponding meter?

> Half a league, half a league
> Half a league onward,
> All in the valley of Death
> Rode the six hundred.
> 'Forward, the Light Brigade!
> Charge for the guns!' he said:
> Into the valley of Death
> Rode the six hundred.—Alfred Lord Tennyson *"The Charge of the Light Brigade"*

    a. Iambic (unstressed/stressed syllables)
    b. Anapest (unstressed/unstressed/stressed syllables)
    c. Spondee (stressed/stressed syllables)
    d. Dactyl (stressed/unstressed/unstressed syllables)

5. This work, published in 1922, was a modernist piece that was banned both in the United States and overseas for meeting the criteria of obscenity. Taking place in a single day (June 16th, 1904), the novel contains eighteen episodes reflecting the activities of character Leopold Bloom in Dublin, Ireland. Originally written as to portray an Odysseus figure for adults, the structure of the work is often viewed as convoluted and chaotic, as its author utilized the stream of consciousness technique. Its literary reception was vastly polarized and remains so to this day, although modern critics tend to hail the novel as addressing the vast panoramic of futility within contemporary history.

The above passage describes which famous literary work?
    a. James Joyce's *Ulysses*
    b. Anne Sexton's poem "45 Mercy Street"
    c. F. Scott Fitzgerald's *Tender is the Night*
    d. George Eliot's *Middlemarch: A Study of Provincial Life*

6. In 1889, Jerome K. Jerome wrote a humorous account of a boating holiday. Originally intended as a chapter in a serious travel guide, the work became a prime example of a comic novel. Read the passage below, noting the word/words in italics. Answer the question that follows.

> I felt rather hurt about this at first; it seemed somehow to be a sort of slight. Why hadn't I got housemaid's knee? Why this invidious reservation? After a while, however, less grasping feelings prevailed. I reflected that I had every other known malady in the pharmacology, and I grew less selfish, and determined to do without housemaid's knee. Gout, in its most malignant stage, it would appear, had seized me without my being aware of it; and *zymosis* I had evidently been suffering with from boyhood. There were no more diseases after *zymosis*, so I concluded there was nothing else the matter with me.—Jerome K. Jerome, *Three Men in a Boat*

Which definition best fits the word *zymosis*?
    a. Discontent
    b. An infectious disease
    c. Poverty
    d. Bad luck

7. Read the following poem. Which option best describes the use of the spider?

> The spider as an artist
> Has never been employed
> Though his surpassing merit
> Is freely certified
> By every broom and Bridget
> Throughout a Christian land.
> Neglected son of genius,
> I take thee by the hand—Emily Dickinson, "Cobwebs"

    a. Idiom
    b. Haiku
    c. ABBA rhyming convention
    d. Simile

8. Which of the following is a pre-reading strategy used to support comprehension?
    a. Skimming the text for content
    b. Summarizing the text effectively
    c. Organizing the main ideas and supporting details
    d. Clarifying unfamiliar ideas in the text

9. Which best describes the *plot* in fiction?
    a. What happens in the story or the storyline
    b. Character development
    c. The time and place of the story
    d. The events in the story that are true

10. Which option best portrays *second person point of view*?
    a. I went down the road, hoping to catch a glimpse of his retreating figure.
    b. You, my dear reader, can understand loss and grief, too.
    c. He left her standing there, alone to face the world.
    d. There's nothing wrong with Margaret.

11. Which option best defines a *fable*?
    a. A melancholy poem lamenting its subject's death
    b. An oral tradition influenced by culture
    c. A story with events that occur in threes and in sevens
    d. A short story with animals, fantastic creatures, or other forces within nature

12. Which of the following describes the organizational pattern of chronological or sequence order?
    a. Text organized by describing a dilemma and a possible solution
    b. Text organized by observing the consequences of an action
    c. Text organized by the timing of events or actions
    d. Text organized by analyzing the relative placement of an object or event

13. Which phrase best completes the definition of a *memoir*?
    a. A historical account of a person's life written by one who has intimate knowledge of the person's life
    b. A historical account of a person's life written by the person himself or herself
    c. A fictional account about a famous person
    d. A nonfictional account about a famous person without factual reference

14. Which of the following is an example of a rhetorical strategy?
    a. Cause and effect
    b. Antimetabole
    c. Individual vs. Self
    d. Ad hominem

15. Which poem belongs to the metaphysical literary movement?
    a. Emily Dickinson's "If I Should Die"
    b. Elizabeth Barrett Browning's "A Child Asleep"
    c. Andrew Marvell's "To His Coy Mistress"
    d. Sylvia Plath's "The Bell Jar"

16. Which word serves as the best example of the poetic device, *onomatopoeia*?
    a. Crackle
    b. Eat
    c. Provide
    d. Walking

17. Which term best defines a *sonnet*?
    a. A Japanese love poem
    b. An eight-line stanza or poem
    c. A fourteen-line poem written in iambic pentameter
    d. A ceremonious, lyric poem

18. Which literary school of thought developed out of structuralism in the twentieth century?
    a. Deconstruction
    b. Post-Structuralism
    c. Marxism
    d. Both A and B

19. Which phrase below best defines *inference*?
    a. Reading between the lines
    b. Skimming a text for context clues
    c. Writing notes or questions that need answers during the reading experience
    d. Summarizing the text

20. Which word best defines the prior knowledge a reader brings to the reading?
    a. Meta-cognitive
    b. Foreshadowing
    c. Schema
    d. Prediction

21. Which phrase best describes the purpose of nonfiction writing?
    a. To inform, entertain, or persuade readers
    b. To entertain, then to inform
    c. To convince readers they're wrong about the author's subject
    d. None of the above

22. Which phrase best defines *connotation*?
    a. An author's use of footnotes in his or her informational text
    b. Words or phrases that mean exactly what they say
    c. The author's use of allusion
    d. When an author chooses words or phrases that invoke feelings rather than a literal meaning

23. Which phrase below best defines the term *audience* as it is used in rhetoric?
    a. The group of readers to which the author is trying to appeal
    b. Students
    c. Subject matter experts
    d. Readers who already have formed subject matter opinions

24. Which of the below definitions is applicable to the *slippery slope* fallacy?
    a. Misrepresenting someone's argument
    b. Asserting that if one event occurs, the rest must follow as natural consequence
    c. Personal attack
    d. Using the opinion of the majority to sway the reader

25. How is it best for readers to approach non-print media critically?
    a. Assume sound bites are generally accurate
    b. Exclude printed text when approaching non-print media
    c. Become a subject matter expert on the topic at hand
    d. Address additional sources and not exclude printed text upon viewing non-print media

Answer Explanations

1. D: Choice *D* correctly summarizes Frost's theme of life's journey and the choices one makes. While Choice *A* can be seen as an interpretation, it is a literal one and is incorrect. Literal is not symbolic. Choice *B* presents the idea of good and evil as a theme, and the poem does not specify this struggle for the traveler. Choice *C* is a similarly incorrect answer. Love is not the theme.

2. B: Only Choice *B* uses both repetitive beginning sounds (alliteration) and personification—the portrayal of a building as a human crumbling under a fire. Choice *A* is a simile and does not utilize alliteration or the use of consistent consonant sounds for effect. Choice *C* is a metaphor and does not utilize alliteration. Choice *D* describes neither alliteration nor personification.

3. B: The correct answer is ABAB. Choice *A* is not a valid rhyme scheme. Choice *C* would require the second and third lines to rhyme, so it is incorrect. Choice *D* would require the first and fifth lines rhyme, then the second and sixth. This is also incorrect as the passage only contains four lines.

4. D: The correct answer is dactyl. If read with the combination of stressed and unstressed syllables as Tennyson intended and as the poem naturally flows, the reader will stumble upon the stressed/unstressed/unstressed rhythmic, dactyl meter similar to a waltz beat. Choices *A*, *B*, and *C* describe meters that do not follow the dactyl pattern.

5. A: The correct answer is *A* as it is the only option that utilizes stream of consciousness technique in a novel format. Choice *B* is a poem by poet Anne Sexton, not a novel. Although Ms. Sexton's works were often criticized for their intimate content, this answer does not meet the question's criteria. Choices *C* and *D* are both incorrect. Both are novels, but not of the appropriate time period, country, or literary content.

6. B: The correct answer is an infectious disease. By reading and understanding the context of the passage, all other options can be eliminated since the author restates zymosis as a disease.

7. D: The correct answer is simile. Choice *A* is incorrect because the poem does not contain an idiom. Choice *B* is incorrect since the poem is not haiku. Choice *C* is incorrect as it does not use the ABBA rhyming convention.

8. A: The correct answer is skimming the text for content. Skimming text for content is an important pre-reading strategy where readers identify important ideas and words without reading every line of the text. Summarizing text effectively, organizing main ideas and supporting details, and clarifying unfamiliar ideas in the text are all reading strategies to be used during or after reading a text.

9. A: The correct answer is "what happens" or the storyline. Choice *B* refers to characters in fiction. Choice *C* defines the setting. Choice *D* is incomplete. It may be partially true, but it isn't always the case. Most fiction is based on the imaginary.

10. B: The correct answer is *B* as the author is speaking directly to the reader and uses the pronoun *you*. Choice *A* uses first person point of view, which uses the pronoun *I*. Choice *C* uses third person point of view which utilizes pronouns such as *he*, *she*, or *we*. Choice *D* is unclear.

11. D: The correct answer is a short story with animals, fantastic creatures, or other forces within nature. Choice *A* defines an elegy. Choice *B* partially alludes to folklore. Choice *C* defines a fairytale.

12. C: The correct answer is text organized by the timing of events or actions. Chronological or sequence order is the organizational pattern that structures text to show the passage of time or movement through steps in a certain order. Choice *A* demonstrates the problem/solution structure. Choice *B* defines the cause/effect pattern. Choice *D* represents the spatial order structure.

13. A: The correct answer is a historical account of a person's life written by one who has intimate knowledge of the person's life. Choice *B* is not applicable since it is the definition of an autobiography. Choice *C* strictly refers to fiction and is not applicable to nonfiction. Choice *D* indicates that a memoir is not based on historical fact. In many instances, it is.

14. A: The correct answer is cause and effect. A writer may use cause and effect as a strategy to illustrate a point in order to convince an audience. Choice *B* is a rhetorical device, not a strategy. Choice *C* refers to a narrative conflict, and Choice *D* is a logical fallacy.

15. C: The correct answer is Andrew Marvell's "To His Coy Mistress." Emily Dickinson, Elizabeth Barrett Browning, and Sylvia Plath all belonged to different literary movements and contexts.

16. A: The correct answer is *crackle* as it is the only option that reflects the sound that the action would make. The other options do not.

17. C: The correct answer is a fourteen-line poem written in iambic pentameter. Choice *A* is incorrect as it incorrectly alludes to the haiku form. Choice *B* defines the octave poetic structure. Choice *D* defines what a poetic ode is.

18. D: The correct answer is that both Deconstruction and Post-structuralism developed in response to the Structuralism movement of the twentieth century. Choices *A* and *B* are incomplete answers as they do not complete both literary movements which encapsulate the response to Structuralism. Choice *C* is incorrect as Marxism was a response to the writings of Karl Marx and not in direct response to Structuralism.

19. A: Inferring is reading between the lines. Choice *B* describes the skimming technique. Choice *C* describes a questioning technique readers should employ, and Choice *D* is a simple statement regarding summary. It's an incomplete answer and not applicable to inference.

20. C: The correct answer is schema. Choice *A* is the name of a research-based strategy that asks the reader to decode text passages. Choice *B* is a literary device. Choice *D* is incorrect. It is part of reading instruction strategy, but not entirely applicable to a reader's prior knowledge he or she brings to the experience.

21. A: The correct answer is to inform, entertain, or persuade readers. Choice *B* may be partly true, but it is not wholly true. Choices *C* and *D* are incorrect.

22. D: The correct answer is when an author chooses words or phrases that invoke feelings other than their literal meaning. Choice *A* refers to footnoting, which isn't applicable, and Choice *C* refers to a literary device. Choice *B* defines denotation, which is conceptually the opposite of connotation.

23. A: The correct answer is the group of readers to which the author is trying to appeal. Choice *B* could be a partial answer, but it is incorrect. Choice *C* assumes authors only write for experts, so it is incorrect. Choice *D* is not true. Rhetoric tries to appeal to readers and tries to convince them of a thesis.

24. B: The correct answer is asserting that if one event occurs, the rest must follow as natural consequence. Choice *A* defines the strawman fallacy. Choice *C* alludes to ad hominem. Choice *D* defines the bandwagon fallacy.

25. D: The correct answer is to address additional sources and not exclude printed text when viewing non-print media. Choice *A* is an incorrect statement; readers should never assume sound bites are accurate. Choice *B* is also incorrect. Excluding print media when viewing non-print media is not being a careful consumer. Choice *C* is unlikely to occur.

Language Use and Vocabulary

Understanding the Conventions of Standard English

Parts of Speech
The English language has eight parts of speech, each serving a different grammatical function.

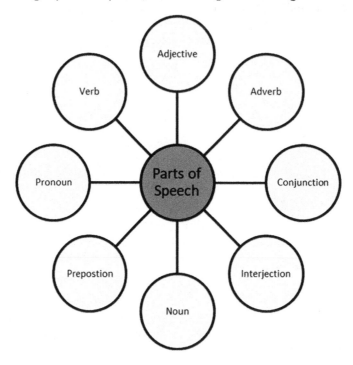

Verb
Verbs describe an action—e.g., *run, play, eat*—or a state of being—e.g., *is, are, was*. It is impossible to make a grammatically-complete sentence without a verb.

> He *runs* to the store.

> She *is* eight years old.

Noun
Nouns can be a person, place, or thing. They can refer to concrete objects—e.g., chair, apple, house—or abstract things—love, knowledge, friendliness.

> Look at the *dog*!

> Where are my *keys*?

Some nouns are *countable*, meaning they can be counted as separate entities—one chair, two chairs, three chairs. They can be either singular or plural. Other nouns, usually substances or concepts, are

uncountable—e.g., air, information, wealth—and some nouns can be both countable and uncountable depending on how they are used.

> I bought three *dresses*.

> *Respect* is important to me.

> I ate way too much *food* last night.

> At the international festival, you can sample *foods* from around the world.

Proper nouns are the specific names of people, places, or things and are almost always capitalized.

> <u>Marie Curie</u> studied at the <u>Flying University</u> in <u>Warsaw, Poland</u>.

Pronoun

Pronouns function as substitutes for nouns or noun phrases. Pronouns are often used to avoid constant repetition of a noun or to simplify sentences. *Personal pronouns* are used for people. Some pronouns are *subject pronouns*; they are used to replace the subject in a sentence—I, we, he, she, they.

> Is *he* your friend?

> *We* work together.

Object pronouns can function as the object of a sentence—me, us, him, her, them.

> Give the documents to *her*.

> Did you call *him* back yet?

Some pronouns can function as either the subject or the object—e.g., you, it. The subject of a sentence is the noun of the sentence that is doing or being something.

> *You* should try it.

> *It* tastes great.

Possessive pronouns indicate ownership. They can be used alone—mine, yours, his, hers, theirs, ours—or with a noun—my, your, his, her, their, ours. In the latter case, they function as a determiner, which is described in detail in the below section on adjectives.

> This table is *ours*.

> I can't find *my* phone!

Reflexive pronouns refer back to the person being spoken or written about. These pronouns end in -*self/-selves*.

> I've heard that New York City is gorgeous in the autumn, but I've never seen it for *myself*.

> After moving away from home, young people have to take care of *themselves*.

Indefinite pronouns are used for things that are unknown or unspecified. Some examples are *anybody, something,* and *everything*.

> I'm looking for *someone* who knows how to fix computers.

> I wanted to buy some shoes today, but I couldn't find *any* that I liked.

Adjective

An adjective modifies a noun, making it more precise or giving more information about it. Adjectives answer these questions: What kind? Which one?

> I just bought a *red* car.

> I don't like *cold* weather.

One special type of word that modifies a noun is a *determiner.* In fact, some grammarians classify determiners as a separate part of speech because whereas adjectives simply describe additional qualities of a noun, a determiner is often a necessary part of a noun phrase, without which the phrase is grammatically incomplete. A determiner indicates whether a noun is definite or indefinite, and can identify which noun is being discussed. It also introduces context to the noun in terms of quantity and possession. The most commonly-used determiners are articles—a, an, the.

> I ordered *a* pizza.

> She lives in *the* city.

Possessive pronouns discussed above, such as *my, your,* and *our,* are also determiners, along with *demonstratives*—this, that—and *quantifiers*—much, many, some. These determiners can take the place of an article.

> Are you using *this* chair?

> I need *some* coffee!

Adverb

Adverbs modify verbs, adjectives, and other adverbs. Words that end in –ly are usually adverbs. Adverbs answer these questions: When? Where? In what manner? To what degree?

> She talks *quickly*.

> The mountains are *incredibly* beautiful!

> The students arrived *early*.

> Please take your phone call *outside*.

Preposition

Prepositions show the relationship between different elements in a phrase or sentence and connect nouns or pronouns to other words in the sentence. Some examples of prepositions are words such as *after, at, behind, by, during, from, in, on, to,* and *with.*

Let's go *to* class.

Starry Night was painted *by* Vincent van Gogh *in* 1889.

Conjunction

Conjunctions join words, phrases, clauses, or sentences together, indicating the type of connection between these elements.

I like pizza, *and* I enjoy spaghetti.

I like to play baseball, *but* I'm allergic to mitts.

Some conjunctions are *coordinating*, meaning they give equal emphasis to two main clauses. Coordinating conjunctions are short, simple words that can be remembered using the mnemonic FANBOYS: for, and, nor, but, or, yet, so. Other conjunctions are *subordinating*. Subordinating conjunctions introduce dependent clauses and include words such as *because, since, before, after, if,* and *while.*

Interjection

An *interjection* is a short word that shows greeting or emotion. Examples of interjections include *wow, ouch, hey, oops, alas,* and *hey.*

Wow! Look at that sunset!

Was it your birthday yesterday? *Oops*! I forgot.

Errors in Standard English Grammar, Usage, Syntax, and Mechanics

Sentence Fragments

A *complete sentence* requires a verb and a subject that expresses a complete thought. Sometimes, the subject is omitted in the case of the implied *you*, used in sentences that are the command or imperative form—e.g., "Look!" or "Give me that." It is understood that the subject of the command is *you*, the listener or reader, so it is possible to have a structure without an explicit subject. Without these elements, though, the sentence is incomplete—it is a *sentence fragment*. While sentence fragments often occur in conversational English or creative writing, they are generally not appropriate in academic writing. Sentence fragments often occur when dependent clauses are not joined to an independent clause:

Sentence fragment: Because the airline overbooked the flight.

The sentence above is a dependent clause that does not express a complete thought. What happened as a result of this cause? With the addition of an independent clause, this now becomes a complete sentence:

> *Complete sentence*: Because the airline overbooked the flight, several passengers were unable to board.

Sentences fragments may also occur through improper use of conjunctions:

> I'm going to the Bahamas for spring break. And to New York City for New Year's Eve.

While the first sentence above is a complete sentence, the second one is not because it is a prepositional phrase that lacks a subject [I] and a verb [am going]. Joining the two together with the coordinating conjunction forms one grammatically-correct sentence:

> I'm going to the Bahamas for spring break and to New York City for New Year's Eve.

Run-ons
A *run-on* is a sentence with too many independent clauses that are improperly connected to each other:

> This winter has been very cold some farmers have suffered damage to their crops.

The sentence above has two subject-verb combinations. The first is "this winter has been"; the second is "some farmers have suffered." However, they are simply stuck next to each other without any punctuation or conjunction. Therefore, the sentence is a run-on.

Another type of run-on occurs when writers use inappropriate punctuation:

> This winter has been very cold, some farmers have suffered damage to their crops.

Though a comma has been added, this sentence is still not correct. When a comma alone is used to join two independent clauses, it is known as a **comma splice**. Without an appropriate conjunction, a comma cannot join two independent clauses by itself.

Run-on sentences can be corrected by either dividing the independent clauses into two or more separate sentences or inserting appropriate conjunctions and/or punctuation. The run-on sentence can be amended by separating each subject-verb pair into its own sentence:

> This winter has been very cold. Some farmers have suffered damage to their crops.

The run-on can also be fixed by adding a comma and conjunction to join the two independent clauses with each other:

> This winter has been very cold, so some farmers have suffered damage to their crops.

Parallelism
Parallel structure occurs when phrases or clauses within a sentence contain the same structure. Parallelism increases readability and comprehensibility because it is easy to tell which sentence elements are paired with each other in meaning.

> Jennifer enjoys cooking, knitting, and to spend time with her cat.

This sentence is not parallel because the items in the list appear in two different forms. Some are *gerunds*, which is the verb + ing: *cooking, knitting*. The other item uses the *infinitive* form, which is to + verb: *to spend*. To create parallelism, all items in the list may reflect the same form:

> Jennifer enjoys cooking, knitting, and spending time with her cat.

All of the items in the list are now in gerund forms, so this sentence exhibits parallel structure. Here's another example:

> The company is looking for employees who are responsible and with a lot of experience.

Again, the items that are listed in this sentence are not parallel. "Responsible" is an adjective, yet "with a lot of experience" is a prepositional phrase. The sentence elements do not utilize parallel parts of speech.

> The company is looking for employees who are responsible and experienced.

"Responsible" and "experienced" are both adjectives, so this sentence now has parallel structure.

Dangling and Misplaced Modifiers

Modifiers enhance meaning by clarifying or giving greater detail about another part of a sentence. However, incorrectly-placed modifiers have the opposite effect and can cause confusion. A *misplaced modifier* is a modifier that is not located appropriately in relation to the word or phrase that it modifies:

> Because he was one of the greatest thinkers of Renaissance Italy, John idolized Leonardo da Vinci.

In this sentence, the modifier is "because he was one of the greatest thinkers of Renaissance Italy," and the noun it is intended to modify is "Leonardo da Vinci." However, due to the placement of the modifier next to the subject, John, it seems as if the sentence is stating that John was a Renaissance genius, not Da Vinci.

> John idolized Leonard da Vinci because he was one of the greatest thinkers of Renaissance Italy.

The modifier is now adjacent to the appropriate noun, clarifying which of the two men in this sentence is the greatest thinker.

Dangling modifiers modify a word or phrase that is not readily apparent in the sentence. That is, they "dangle" because they are not clearly attached to anything:

> After getting accepted to college, Amir's parents were proud.

The modifier here, "after getting accepted to college," should modify who got accepted. The noun immediately following the modifier is "Amir's parents"—but they are probably not the ones who are going to college.

> After getting accepted to college, Amir made his parents proud.

The subject of the sentence has been changed to Amir himself, and now the subject and its modifier are appropriately matched.

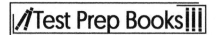

Inconsistent Verb Tense

Verb tense reflects when an action occurred or a state existed. For example, the tense known as *simple present* expresses something that is happening right now or that happens regularly:

> She *works* in a hospital.

Present continuous tense expresses something in progress. It is formed by to be + verb + -ing.

> Sorry, I can't go out right now. I *am doing* my homework.

Past tense is used to describe events that previously occurred. However, in conversational English, speakers often use present tense or a mix of past and present tense when relating past events because it gives the narrative a sense of immediacy. In formal written English, though, consistency in verb tense is necessary to avoid reader confusion.

> I traveled to Europe last summer. As soon as I stepped off the plane, I feel like I'm in a movie! I'm surrounded by quaint cafes and impressive architecture.

The passage above abruptly switches from past tense—*traveled*, *stepped*—to present tense—*feel*, *am surrounded*.

> I *traveled* to Europe last summer. As soon as I *stepped* off the plane, I *felt* like I was in a movie! I *was surrounded* by quaint cafes and impressive architecture.

All verbs are in past tense, so this passage now has consistent verb tense.

Split Infinitives

The *infinitive form* of a verb consists of "to + base verb"—e.g., to walk, to sleep, to approve. A *split infinitive* occurs when another word, usually an adverb, is placed between *to* and the verb:

> I decided *to simply walk* to work to get more exercise every day.

The infinitive *to walk* is split by the adverb *simply*.

> It was a mistake *to hastily approve* the project before conducting further preliminary research.

The infinitive *to approve* is split by *hastily*.

Although some grammarians still advise against split infinitives, this syntactic structure is common in both spoken and written English and is widely accepted in standard usage.

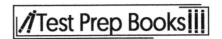

Subject-Verb Agreement

In English, verbs must agree with the subject. The form of a verb may change depending on whether the subject is singular or plural, or whether it is first, second, or third person. For example, the verb *to be* has various forms:

> I <u>am</u> a student.

> You <u>are</u> a student.

> She <u>is</u> a student.

> We <u>are</u> students.

> They <u>are</u> students.

Errors occur when a verb does not agree with its subject. Sometimes, the error is readily apparent:

> We is hungry.

Is is not the appropriate form of *to be* when used with the third person plural *we*.

> We are hungry.

This sentence now has correct subject-verb agreement.

However, some cases are trickier, particularly when the subject consists of a lengthy noun phrase with many modifiers:

> Students who are hoping to accompany the anthropology department on its annual summer trip to Ecuador needs to sign up by March 31st.

The verb in this sentence is *needs*. However, its subject is not the noun adjacent to it—Ecuador. The subject is the noun at the beginning of the sentence—students. Because *students* is plural, *needs* is the incorrect verb form.

> *Students* who are hoping to accompany the anthropology department on its annual summer trip to Ecuador *need* to sign up by March 31st.

This sentence now uses correct agreement between *students* and *need*.

Another case to be aware of is a *collective noun*. A collective noun refers to a group of many things or people but can be singular in itself—e.g., family, committee, army, pair team, council, jury. Whether or not a collective noun uses a singular or plural verb depends on how the noun is being used. If the noun refers to the group performing a collective action as one unit, it should use a singular verb conjugation:

> The family is moving to a new neighborhood.

The whole family is moving together in unison, so the singular verb form *is* is appropriate here.

> The committee has made its decision.

The verb *has* and the possessive pronoun *its* both reflect the word *committee* as a singular noun in the sentence above; however, when a collective noun refers to the group as individuals, it can take a plural verb:

> The newlywed pair spend every moment together.

This sentence emphasizes the love between two people in a pair, so it can use the plural verb *spend*.

> The council are all newly elected members.

The sentence refers to the council in terms of its individual members and uses the plural verb *are*.

Overall though, American English is more likely to pair a collective noun with a singular verb, while British English is more likely to pair a collective noun with a plural verb.

Grammar, Usage, Syntax, and Mechanics Choices

Colons and Semicolons

In a sentence, *colons* are used before a list, a summary or elaboration, or an explanation related to the preceding information in the sentence:

> There are two ways to reserve tickets for the performance: by phone or in person.

> One thing is clear: students are spending more on tuition than ever before.

As these examples show, a colon must be preceded by an independent clause. However, the information after the colon may be in the form of an independent clause or in the form of a list.

Semicolons can be used in two different ways—to join ideas or to separate them. In some cases, semicolons can be used to connect what would otherwise be stand-alone sentences. Each part of the sentence joined by a semicolon must be an independent clause. The use of a semicolon indicates that these two independent clauses are closely related to each other:

> The rising cost of childcare is one major stressor for parents; healthcare expenses are another source of anxiety.

> Classes have been canceled due to the snowstorm; check the school website for updates.

Semicolons can also be used to divide elements of a sentence in a more distinct way than simply using a comma. This usage is particularly useful when the items in a list are especially long and complex and contain other internal punctuation.

> Retirees have many modes of income: some survive solely off their retirement checks; others supplement their income through part time jobs, like working in a supermarket or substitute teaching; and others are financially dependent on the support of family members, friends, and spouses.

Its and It's

These pronouns are some of the most confused in the English language as most possessives contain the suffix —'s. However, for *it*, it is the opposite. *Its* is a possessive pronoun:

> The government is reassessing *its* spending plan.

It's is a contraction of the words *it is*:

> *It's* snowing outside.

Saw and Seen

Saw and *seen* are both conjugations of the verb *to see*, but they express different verb tenses. *Saw* is used in the simple past tense. *Seen* is the past participle form of *to see* and can be used in all perfect tenses.

> I seen her yesterday.

This sentence is incorrect. Because it expresses a completed event from a specified point in time in the past, it should use simple past tense:

> I *saw* her yesterday.

This sentence uses the correct verb tense. Here's how the past participle is used correctly:

> I *have seen* her before.

The meaning in this sentence is slightly changed to indicate an event from an unspecific time in the past. In this case, present perfect is the appropriate verb tense to indicate an unspecified past experience. Present perfect conjugation is created by combining *to have* + past participle.

Then and Than

Then is generally used as an adverb indicating something that happened next in a sequence or as the result of a conditional situation:

> We parked the car and *then* walked to the restaurant.

> If enough people register for the event, *then* we can begin planning.

Than is a conjunction indicating comparison:

> This watch is more expensive *than* that one.

> The bus departed later *than* I expected.

They're, Their, and There

They're is a contraction of the words *they are*:

> *They're* moving to Ohio next week.

Their is a possessive pronoun:

> The baseball players are training for *their* upcoming season.

There can function as multiple parts of speech, but it is most commonly used as an adverb indicating a location:

> Let's go to the concert! Some great bands are playing *there*.

Insure and Ensure

These terms are both verbs. *Insure* means to guarantee something against loss, harm, or damage, usually through an insurance policy that offers monetary compensation:

> The robbers made off with her prized diamond necklace, but luckily it was *insured* for one million dollars.

Ensure means to make sure, to confirm, or to be certain:

> *Ensure* that you have your passport before entering the security checkpoint.

Accept and Except

Accept is a verb meaning to take or agree to something:

> I would like to *accept* your offer of employment.

Except is a preposition that indicates exclusion:

> I've been to every state in America *except* Hawaii.

Affect and Effect

Affect is a verb meaning to influence or to have an impact on something:

> The amount of rainfall during the growing season *affects* the flavor of wine produced from these grapes.

Effect can be used as either a noun or a verb. As a noun, *effect* is synonymous with a result:

> If we implement the changes, what will the *effect* be on our profits?

As a verb, *effect* means to bring about or to make happen:

> In just a few short months, the healthy committee has *effected* real change in school nutrition.

Components of Sentences

Clauses

Clauses contain a subject and a verb. An *independent clause* can function as a complete sentence on its own, but it might also be one component of a longer sentence. *Dependent clauses* cannot stand alone as complete sentences. They rely on independent clauses to complete their meaning. Dependent clauses usually begin with a subordinating conjunction. Independent and dependent clauses are sometimes also referred to as *main clauses* and *subordinate clauses*, respectively. The following structure highlights the differences:

> Apiculturists raise honeybees because they love insects.

Apiculturists raise honeybees is an independent or main clause. The subject is *apiculturists*, and the verb is *raise*. It expresses a complete thought and could be a standalone sentence.

Because they love insects is a dependent or subordinate clause. If it were not attached to the independent clause, it would be a sentence fragment. While it contains a subject and verb—*they love*—this clause is dependent because it begins with the subordinate conjunction *because*. Thus, it does not express a complete thought on its own.

Another type of clause is a *relative clause*, and it is sometimes referred to as an *adjective clause* because it gives further description about the noun. A relative clause begins with a *relative pronoun*: *that, which, who, whom, whichever, whomever,* or *whoever.* It may also begin with a *relative adverb*: *where, why,* or *when.* Here's an example of a relative clause, functioning as an adjective:

The strawberries that I bought yesterday are already beginning to spoil.

Here, the relative clause is *that I bought yesterday*; the relative pronoun is *that*. The subject is *I*, and the verb is *bought*. The clause modifies the subject *strawberries* by answering the question, "Which strawberries?" Here's an example of a relative clause with an adverb:

The tutoring center is a place where students can get help with homework.

The relative clause is *where students can get help with homework*, and it gives more information about a place by describing what kind of place it is. It begins with the relative adverb *where* and contains the noun *students* along with its verb phrase *can get*.

Relative clauses may be further divided into two types: essential or nonessential. *Essential clauses* contain identifying information without which the sentence would lose significant meaning or not make sense. These are also sometimes referred to as *restrictive clauses*. The sentence above contains an example of an essential relative clause. Here is what happens when the clause is removed:

The tutoring center is a place where students can get help with homework.

The tutoring center is a place.

Without the relative clause, the sentence loses the majority of its meaning; thus, the clause is essential or restrictive.

Nonessential clauses—also referred to as *non-restrictive clauses*—offer additional information about a noun in the sentence, but they do not significantly control the overall meaning of the sentence. The following example indicates a nonessential clause:

New York City, which is located in the northeastern part of the country, is the most populated city in America.

New York City is the most populated city in America.

Even without the relative clause, the sentence is still understandable and continues to communicate its central message about New York City. Thus, it is a nonessential clause.

Punctuation differs between essential and nonessential relative clauses, too. Nonessential clauses are set apart from the sentence using commas whereas essential clauses are not separated with commas.

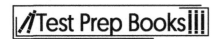

Also, the relative pronoun *that* is generally used for essential clauses, while *which* is used for nonessential clauses. The following examples clarify this distinction:

> *Romeo and Juliet* is my favorite play *that Shakespeare wrote.*

The relative clause *that Shakespeare wrote* contains essential, controlling information about the noun *play*, limiting it to those plays by Shakespeare. Without it, it would seem that *Romeo and Juliet* is the speaker's favorite play out of every play ever written, not simply from Shakespeare's repertoire.

> *Romeo and Juliet, which Shakespeare wrote*, is my favorite play.

Here, the nonessential relative clause—"which Shakespeare wrote"—modifies *Romeo and Juliet*. It doesn't provide controlling information about the play, but simply offers further background details. Thus, commas are needed.

Phrases

Phrases are groups of words that do not contain the subject-verb combination required for clauses. Phrases are classified by the part of speech that begins or controls the phrase.

A *noun phrase* consists of a noun and all its modifiers—adjectives, adverbs, and determiners. Noun phrases can serve many functions in a sentence, acting as subjects, objects, and object complements:

> *The shallow yellow bowl* sits on the top shelf.

> Nina just bought *some incredibly fresh organic produce.*

Prepositional phrases are made up of a preposition and its object. The object of a preposition might be a noun, noun phrase, pronoun, or gerund. Prepositional phrases may function as either an adjective or an adverb:

> Jack picked up the book *in front of him.*

The prepositional phrase *in front of him* acts as an adjective indicating which book Jack picked up.

> The dog ran into the back yard.

The phrase *into the backyard* describes where the dog ran, so it acts as an adverb.

Verb phrases include all of the words in a verb group, even if they are not directly adjacent to each other:

> I *should have woken up* earlier this morning.

> The company **is** now *offering* membership discounts for new enrollers.

This sentence's verb phrase is *is offering*. Even though they are separated by the word *now*, they function together as a single verb phrase.

Structures of Sentences

All sentences contain the same basic elements: a subject and a verb. The *subject* is who or what the sentence is about; the *verb* describes the subject's action or condition. However, these elements,

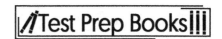

subjects and verbs, can be combined in different ways. The following graphic describes the different types of sentence structures.

Sentence Structure	Independent Clauses	Dependent Clauses
Simple	1	0
Compound	2 or more	0
Complex	1	1 or more
Compound-Complex	2 or more	1 or more

A *simple sentence* expresses a complete thought and consists of one subject and verb combination:

> The children ate pizza.

The subject is *children*. The verb is *ate*.

Either the subject or the verb may be *compound*—that is, it could have more than one element:

> *The children and their parents* ate pizza.

> The children *ate pizza and watched a movie.*

All of these are still simple sentences. Despite having either compound subjects or compound verbs, each sentence still has only one subject and verb combination.

Compound sentences combine two or more simple sentences to form one sentence that has multiple subject-verb combinations:

> *The children ate pizza,* and *their parents watched a movie.*

This structure is comprised of two independent clauses: (1) *the children ate pizza* and (2) *their parents watched a movie.* Compound sentences join different subject-verb combinations using a comma and a coordinating conjunction.

> I called my mom**,** *but* she didn't answer the phone.

> The weather was stormy**,** *so* we canceled our trip to the beach.

A *complex sentence* consists of an independent clause and one or more dependent clauses. Dependent clauses join a sentence using *subordinating conjunctions*. Some examples of subordinating conjunctions are *although*, *unless*, *as soon as*, *since*, *while*, *when*, *because*, *if*, and *before*.

> I missed class yesterday *because* my mother was ill.

> *Before* traveling to a new country, you need to exchange your money to the local currency.

The order of clauses determines their punctuation. If the dependent clause comes first, it should be separated from the independent clause with a comma. However, if the complex sentence consists of an independent clause followed by a dependent clause, then a comma is not always necessary.

A *compound-complex sentence* can be created by joining two or more independent clauses with at least one dependent clause:

> After the earthquake struck, thousands of homes were destroyed, and many families were left without a place to live.

The first independent clause in the compound structure includes a dependent clause—*after the earthquake struck*. Thus, the structure is both complex and compound.

Understanding the Use of Affixes, Context, and Syntax

<u>Affixes</u>

Individual words are constructed from building blocks of meaning. An *affix* is an element that is added to a root or stem word that can change the word's meaning.

For example, the stem word *fix* is a verb meaning *to repair*. When the ending *–able* is added, it becomes the adjective *fixable*, meaning "capable of being repaired." Adding *un–* to the beginning changes the word to *unfixable*, meaning "incapable of being repaired." In this way, affixes attach to the word stem to create a new word and a new meaning. Knowledge of affixes can assist in deciphering the meaning of unfamiliar words.

Affixes are also related to inflection. *Inflection* is the modification of a base word to express a different grammatical or syntactical function. For example, countable nouns such as *car* and *airport* become plural with the addition of *–s* at the end: *cars* and *airports*.

Verb tense is also expressed through inflection. *Regular verbs*—those that follow a standard inflection pattern—can be changed to past tense using the affixes *–ed*, *–d*, or *–ied*, as in *cooked* and *studied*. Verbs can also be modified for continuous tenses by using *–ing*, as in *working* or *exploring*. Thus, affixes are used not only to express meaning but also to reflect a word's grammatical purpose.

A *prefix* is an affix attached to the beginning of a word. The meanings of English prefixes mainly come from Greek and Latin origins. The chart below contains a few of the most commonly used English prefixes.

Prefix	Meaning	Example
a-	not	amoral, asymptomatic
anti-	against	antidote, antifreeze
auto-	self	automobile, automatic
circum-	around	circumference, circumspect
co-, com-, con-	together	coworker, companion
contra-	against	contradict, contrary
de-	negation or reversal	deflate, deodorant
extra-	outside, beyond	extraterrestrial, extracurricular
in-, im-, il-, ir-	not	impossible, irregular
inter-	between	international, intervene
intra-	within	intramural, intranet
mis-	wrongly	mistake, misunderstand
mono-	one	monolith, monopoly
non-	not	nonpartisan, nonsense
pre-	before	preview, prediction
re-	again	review, renew
semi-	half	semicircle, semicolon
sub-	under	subway, submarine
super-	above	superhuman, superintendent
trans-	across, beyond, through	trans-Siberian, transform
un-	not	unwelcome, unfriendly

While the addition of a prefix alters the meaning of the base word, the addition of a *suffix* may also affect a word's part of speech. For example, adding a suffix can change the noun *material* into the verb *materialize* and back to a noun again in *materialization*.

Suffix	Part of Speech	Meaning	Example
-able, -ible	adjective	having the ability to	honorable, flexible
-acy, -cy	noun	state or quality	intimacy, dependency
-al, -ical	adjective	having the quality of	historical, tribal
-en	verb	to cause to become	strengthen, embolden
-er, -ier	adjective	comparative	happier, longer
-est, -iest	adjective	superlative	sunniest, hottest
-ess	noun	female	waitress, actress
-ful	adjective	full of, characterized by	beautiful, thankful
-fy, -ify	verb	to cause, to come to be	liquefy, intensify
-ism	noun	doctrine, belief, action	Communism, Buddhism
-ive, -ative, -itive	adjective	having the quality of	creative, innovative
-ize	verb	to convert into, to subject to	Americanize, dramatize
-less	adjective	without, missing	emotionless, hopeless
-ly	adverb	in the manner of	quickly, energetically
-ness	noun	quality or state	goodness, darkness
-ous, -ious, -eous	adjective	having the quality of	spontaneous, pious
-ship	noun	status or condition	partnership, ownership
-tion	noun	action or state	renovation, promotion
-y	adjective	characterized by	smoky, dreamy

Through knowledge of prefixes and suffixes, a student's vocabulary can be instantly expanded with an understanding of *etymology*—the origin of words. This, in turn, can be used to add sentence structure variety to academic writing.

Context Clues
Familiarity with common prefixes, suffixes, and root words assists tremendously in unraveling the meaning of an unfamiliar word and making an educated guess as to its meaning. However, some words do not contain many easily-identifiable clues that point to their meaning. In this case, rather than looking at the elements within the word, it is useful to consider elements around the word—i.e., its context. *Context* refers to the other words and information within the sentence or surrounding sentences that indicate the unknown word's probable meaning. The following sentences provide context for the potentially-unfamiliar word *quixotic*:

Rebecca had never been one to settle into a predictable, ordinary life. Her quixotic personality led her to leave behind a job with a prestigious law firm in Manhattan and move halfway around the world to pursue her dream of becoming a sushi chef in Tokyo.

64

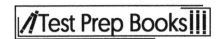

A reader unfamiliar with the word *quixotic* doesn't have many clues to use in terms of affixes or root meaning. The suffix *–ic* indicates that the word is an adjective, but that is it. In this case, then, a reader would need to look at surrounding information to obtain some clues about the word. Other adjectives in the passage include *predictable* and *ordinary*, things that Rebecca was definitely not, as indicated by "Rebecca had never been one to settle." Thus, a first clue might be that *quixotic* means the opposite of predictable.

The second sentence doesn't offer any other modifier of *personality* other than *quixotic*, but it does include a story that reveals further information about her personality. She had a stable, respectable job, but she decided to give it up to follow her dream. Combining these two ideas together, then— unpredictable and dream-seeking—gives the reader a general idea of what *quixotic* probably means. In fact, the root of the word is the character Don Quixote, a romantic dreamer who goes on an impulsive adventure.

While context clues are useful for making an approximate definition for newly-encountered words, these types of clues also come in handy when encountering common words that have multiple meanings. The word *reservation* is used differently in each the following sentences:

A. That restaurant is booked solid for the next month; it's impossible to make a reservation unless you know somebody.

B. The hospital plans to open a branch office inside the reservation to better serve Native American patients who cannot easily travel to the main hospital fifty miles away.

C. Janet Clark is a dependable, knowledgeable worker, and I recommend her for the position of team leader without reservation.

All three sentences use the word to express different meanings. In fact, most words in English have more than one meaning—sometimes meanings that are completely different from one another. Thus, context can provide clues as to which meaning is appropriate in a given situation. A quick search in the dictionary reveals several possible meanings for *reservation*:

1. An exception or qualification
2. A tract of public land set aside, such as for the use of American Indian tribes
3. An arrangement for accommodations, such as in a hotel, on a plane, or at a restaurant

Sentence A mentions a restaurant, making the third definition the correct one in this case. In sentence B, some context clues include Native Americans, as well as the implication that a reservation is a place— "inside the reservation," both of which indicate that the second definition should be used here. Finally, sentence C uses *without reservation* to mean "completely" or "without exception," so the first definition can be applied here.

Using context clues in this way can be especially useful for words that have multiple, widely varying meanings. If a word has more than one definition and two of those definitions are the opposite of each other, it is known as an *auto-antonym*—a word that can also be its own antonym. In the case of auto-antonyms, context clues are crucial to determine which definition to employ in a given sentence. For example, the word *sanction* can either mean "to approve or allow" or "a penalty." Approving and penalizing have opposite meanings, so *sanction* is an example of an auto-antonym.

The following sentences reflect the distinction in meaning:

A. In response to North Korea's latest nuclear weapons test, world leaders have called for harsher sanctions to punish the country for its actions.

B. The general has sanctioned a withdrawal of troops from the area.

A context clue can be found in sentence A, which mentions "to punish." A punishment is similar to a penalty, so sentence A is using the word *sanction* according to this definition.

Other examples of auto-antonyms include *oversight*—"to supervise something" or "a missed detail"), *resign*—"to quit" or "to sign again, as a contract," and *screen*—"to show" or "to conceal." For these types of words, recognizing context clues is an important way to avoid misinterpreting the sentence's meaning.

Syntax

Syntax refers to the arrangement of words, phrases, and clauses to form a sentence. Knowledge of syntax can also give insight into a word's meaning. The section above considered several examples using the word *reservation* and applied context clues to determine the word's appropriate meaning in each sentence. Here is an example of how the placement of a word can impact its meaning and grammatical function:

A. The development team has reserved the conference room for today.

B. Her quiet and reserved nature is sometimes misinterpreted as unfriendliness when people first meet her.

In addition to using *reserved* to mean different things, each sentence also uses the word to serve a different grammatical function. In sentence A, *reserved* is part of the verb phrase *has reserved*, indicating the meaning "to set aside for a particular use." In sentence B, *reserved* acts as a modifier within the noun phrase "her quiet and reserved nature." Because the word is being used as an adjective to describe a personality characteristic, it calls up a different definition of the word—"restrained or lacking familiarity with others." As this example shows, the function of a word within the overall sentence structure can allude to its meaning. It is also useful to refer to the earlier chart about suffixes and parts of speech as another clue into what grammatical function a word is serving in a sentence.

Analyzing Nuances of Word Meaning and Figures of Speech

By now, it should be apparent that language is not as simple as one word directly correlated to one meaning. Rather, one word can express a vast array of diverse meanings, and similar meanings can be expressed through different words. However, there are very few words that express exactly the same meaning. For this reason, it is important to be able to pick up on the nuances of word meaning.

Many words contain two levels of meaning: connotation and denotation as discussed previously in the informational texts and rhetoric section. A word's *denotation* is its most literal meaning—the definition that can readily be found in the dictionary. A word's *connotation* includes all of its emotional and cultural associations.

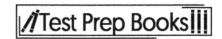

In literary writing, authors rely heavily on connotative meaning to create mood and characterization. The following are two descriptions of a rainstorm:

A. The rain slammed against the windowpane, and the wind howled through the fireplace. A pair of hulking oaks next to the house cast eerie shadows as their branches trembled in the wind.

B. The rain pattered against the windowpane, and the wind whistled through the fireplace. A pair of stately oaks next to the house cast curious shadows as their branches swayed in the wind.

Description A paints a creepy picture for readers with strongly emotional words like *slammed*, connoting force and violence. *Howled* connotes pain or wildness, and *eerie* and *trembled* connote fear. Overall, the connotative language in this description serves to inspire fear and anxiety.

However, as can be seen in description B, swapping out a few key words for those with different connotations completely changes the feeling of the passage. *Slammed* is replaced with the more cheerful *pattered*, and *hulking* has been swapped out for *stately*. Both words imply something large, but *hulking* is more intimidating whereas *stately* is more respectable. *Curious* and *swayed* seem more playful than the language used in the earlier description. Although both descriptions represent roughly the same situation, the nuances of the emotional language used throughout the passages create a very different sense for readers.

Selective choice of connotative language can also be extremely impactful in other forms of writing, such as editorials or persuasive texts. Through connotative language, writers reveal their biases and opinions while trying to inspire feelings and actions in readers:

A. Parents won't stop complaining about standardized tests.
B. Parents continue to raise concerns about standardized tests.

Readers should be able to identify the nuance in meaning between these two sentences. The first one carries a more negative feeling, implying that parents are being bothersome or whiny. Readers of the second sentence, though, might come away with the feeling that parents are concerned and involved in their children's education. Again, the aggregate of even subtle cues can combine to give a specific emotional impression to readers, so from an early age, students should be aware of how language can be used to influence readers' opinions.

Another form of non-literal expression can be found in *figures of speech*. As with connotative language, figures of speech tend to be shared within a cultural group and may be difficult to pick up on for learners outside of that group. In some cases, a figure of speech may be based on the literal denotation of the words it contains, but in other cases, a figure of speech is far removed from its literal meaning. A case in point is *irony*, where what is said is the exact opposite of what is meant:

The new tax plan is poorly planned, based on faulty economic data, and unable to address the financial struggles of middle class families. Yet legislators remain committed to passing this brilliant proposal.

When the writer refers to the proposal as brilliant, the opposite is implied—the plan is "faulty" and "poorly planned." By using irony, the writer means that the proposal is anything but brilliant by using the word in a non-literal sense.

Another figure of speech is *hyperbole*—extreme exaggeration or overstatement. Statements like, "I love you to the moon and back" or "Let's be friends for a million years" utilize hyperbole to convey a greater depth of emotion, without literally committing oneself to space travel or a life of immortality.

Figures of speech may sometimes use one word in place of another. *Synecdoche*, for example, uses a part of something to refer to its whole. The expression "Don't hurt a hair on her head!" implies protecting more than just an individual hair, but rather her entire body. "The art teacher is training a class of Picassos" uses Picasso, one individual notable artist, to stand in for the entire category of talented artists. Another figure of speech using word replacement is *metonymy*, where a word is replaced with something closely associated to it. For example, news reports may use the word "Washington" to refer to the American government or "the crown" to refer to the British monarch.

Using Print and Digital Reference Materials

Appropriate Print or Digital Reference Material
Reference materials are indispensable tools for beginners and experts alike. Becoming a competent English communicator doesn't necessarily mean memorizing every single rule about spelling, grammar, or punctuation—it means knowing where and how to find accurate information about the rules of English usage. Students of English have a wide variety of references materials available to them, and, in an increasingly digitized world, more and more of these materials can be found online or as easily-accessible phone applications. Educators should introduce students to different types of reference materials as well as when and how to use them.

Spell Check
Most word processing software programs come equipped with a spell-checking feature. Web browsers and personal devices like smartphones and tablets may also have a spell checker enabled. *Spell check* automatically detects misspelled words and suggests alternate spellings. Many writers have come to rely on spell check due to its convenience and ease of use. However, there are some caveats to using spell check—it only checks whether a word is spelled correctly, not if it is used correctly. As discussed above, there are numerous examples of commonly-confused words in English, the misuse of which may not be detected by a spell checker. Many word processing programs do integrate spell checking and grammar checking functions, however. Thus, although running a spell check is an important part of reviewing any piece of writing, it should not be the only step of the review process. Further, spell checkers recommend correctly-spelled words based on an approximation of the misspelled word, so writers need to be somewhat close to the correct spelling in order for spell check to be useful.

Dictionary
Dictionaries are readily available in print, digital formats, and as mobile apps. A dictionary offers a wealth of information to users. First, in the absence of spell checking software, a *dictionary* can be used to identify correct spelling and to determine the word's pronunciation—often written using the International Phonetic Alphabet (IPA). Perhaps the best-known feature of a dictionary is its explanation of a word's meanings, as a single word can have multiple definitions. A dictionary organizes these definitions based on their parts of speech and then arranges them from most to least commonly used meanings or from oldest to most modern usage. Many dictionaries also offer information about a word's etymology and usage. With all these functions, then, a dictionary is a basic, essential tool in many situations. Students can turn to a dictionary when they encounter an unfamiliar word or when they see a familiar word used in a new way.

There are many dictionaries to choose from, but perhaps the most highly respected source is the *Oxford English Dictionary* (OED). The OED is a historical dictionary, and as such, all entries include quotes of the word as it has been used throughout history. Users of the OED can get a deeper sense of a word's evolution over time and in different parts of the world. Another standard dictionary in America is *Merriam-Webster*.

Thesaurus

Whereas a dictionary entry lists a word's definitions, a *thesaurus* entry lists a word's *synonyms* and *antonyms*—i.e., words with similar and opposite meanings, respectively. A dictionary can be used to find out what a word means and where it came from, and a thesaurus can be used to understand a word's relationship to other words. A thesaurus can be a powerful vocabulary-building tool. By becoming familiar with synonyms and antonyms, students will be more equipped to use a broad range of vocabulary in their speech and writing. Of course, one thing to be aware of when using a thesaurus is that most words do not have exact synonyms. Rather, there are slight nuances of meaning that can make one word more appropriate than another in a given context. In this case, it is often to the user's advantage to consult a thesaurus side-by-side with a dictionary to confirm any differences in usage between two synonyms. Some digital sources, such as *Dictionary.com*, integrate a dictionary and a thesaurus.

Generally, though, a thesaurus is a useful tool to help writers add variety and precision to their word choice. Consulting a thesaurus can help students elevate their writing to an appropriate academic level by replacing vague or overused words with more expressive or academic ones. Also, word processors often offer a built-in thesaurus, making it easy for writers to look up synonyms and vary word choice as they work.

Glossary

A *glossary* is similar to a dictionary in that it offers an explanation of terms. However, while a dictionary attempts to cover every word in a language, a glossary only focuses on those terms relevant to a specific field. Also, a glossary entry is more likely to offer a longer explanation of a term and its relevance within that field. Glossaries are often found at the back of textbooks or other nonfiction publications in order to explain new or unfamiliar terms to readers. A glossary may also be an entire book on its own that covers all of the essential terms and concepts within a particular profession, field, or other specialized area of knowledge. For learners seeking general definitions of terms from any context, then, a dictionary is an appropriate reference source, but for students of specialized fields, a glossary will usually provide more in-depth information.

Style Manual

Many rules of English usage are standard, but other rules may be more subjective. An example can be seen in the following structures:

A. I went to the store and bought eggs, milk, and bread.
B. I went to the store and bought eggs, milk and bread.

The final comma in a list before *and* or *or* is known as an Oxford comma or serial comma. It is, recommended in some styles, but not in others. To determine the appropriate use of the Oxford comma, writers can consult a style manual.

A *style manual* is a comprehensive collection of guidelines for language use and document formatting. Some fields refer to a common style guide—e.g., the Associated Press or *AP Stylebook*, a standard in

American journalism. Individual organizations may rely on their own house style. Regardless, the purpose of a style manual is to ensure uniformity across all documents. Style manuals explain things such as how to format titles, when to write out numbers or use numerals, and how to cite sources. Because there are many different style guides, students should know how and when to consult an appropriate guide. The Chicago Manual of Style is common in the publication of books and academic journals. The Modern Language Association style (MLA) is another commonly used academic style format, while the American Psychological Association style (APA) may be used for scientific publications. Familiarity with using a style guide is particularly important for students who are college bound or pursuing careers in academic or professional writing.

In the previous examples, the Oxford comma is recommended by the Chicago Manual of Style, so sentence A would be correct if the writer is using this style. But the comma is not recommended by the *AP Stylebook*, so sentence B would be correct if the writer is using the AP style.

General Grammar and Style References
Any language arts textbook should offer general grammatical and stylistic advice to students, but there are a few well-respected texts that can also be used for reference. *Elements of Style* by William Strunk is regularly assigned to students as a guide on effective written communication, including how to avoid common usage mistakes and how to make the most of parallel structure. *Garner's Modern American Usage* by Bryan Garner is another text that guides students on how to achieve precision and understandability in their writing. Whereas other reference sources discussed above tend to address specific language concerns, these types of texts offer a more holistic approach to cultivating effective language skills.

Electronic Resources
With print texts, it is easy to identify the authors and their credentials, as well as the publisher and their reputation. With electronic resources like websites, though, it can be trickier to assess the reliability of information. Students should be alert when gathering information from the Internet. Understanding the significance of website *domains*—which include identification strings of a site—can help. Website domains ending in *.edu* are educational sites and tend to offer more reliable research in their field. A *.org* ending tends to be used by nonprofit organizations and other community groups, *.com* indicates a privately-owned website, and a *.gov* site is run by the government. Websites affiliated with official organizations, research groups, or institutes of learning are more likely to offer relevant, fact-checked, and reliable information.

Identifying Dialect and Diction

Identifying Variation in Dialect and Diction
Language arts educators often seem to be in the position of teaching the "right" way to use English, particularly in lessons about grammar and vocabulary. However, all it takes is back-to-back viewings of speeches by the queen of England and the president of the United States or side-by-side readings of a contemporary poem and one written in the 1600s to come to the conclusion that there is no single, fixed, correct form of spoken or written English. Instead, language varies and evolves across different regions and time periods. It also varies between cultural groups depending on factors such as race, ethnicity, age, and socioeconomic status. Students should come away from a language arts class with more than a strictly prescriptive view of language; they should have an appreciation for its rich diversity.

It is important to understand some key terms in discussing linguistic variety.

Language is a tool for communication. It may be spoken, unspoken—as with body language—written, or codified in other ways. Language is symbolic in the sense that it can describe objects, ideas, and events that are not actually present, have not actually occurred, or only exist in the mind of the speaker. All languages are governed by systematic rules of grammar and semantics. These rules allow speakers to manipulate a finite number of elements, such as sounds or written symbols, to create an infinite number of meanings.

A *dialect* is a distinct variety of a language in terms of patterns of grammar, vocabulary, and/or *phonology*—the sounds used by its speakers—that distinguish it from other forms of that language. Two dialects are not considered separate languages if they are *mutually intelligible*—if speakers of each dialect are able to understand one another. A dialect is not a subordinate version of a language. Examples of English dialects include Scottish English and American Southern English.

By definition, *Standard English* is a dialect. It is one variety of English with its own usage of grammar, vocabulary, and pronunciation. Given that Standard English is taught in schools and used in places like government, journalism, and other professional workplaces, it is often elevated above other English dialects. Linguistically, though, there is nothing that makes Standard English more correct or advanced than other dialects.

A *pidgin* is formed when speakers of different languages begin utilizing a simplified mixture of elements from both languages to communicate with each other. In North America, pidgins occurred when Africans were brought to European colonies as slaves, leading to a mixture of African and European languages. Historically, pidgins also sprung up in areas of international trade. A pidgin is communication born of necessity and lacks the full complexity or standardized rules that govern a language.

When a pidgin becomes widely used and is taught to children as their native language, it becomes a *Creole*. An example is Haitian Creole, a language based on French and including elements of West African languages.

An *accent* is a unique speech pattern, particularly in terms of tone or intonation. Speakers from different regions tend to have different accents, as do learners of English from different native languages. In some cases, accents are mutually intelligible, but in other cases, speakers with different accents might have some difficulty in understanding one another.

Colloquial language is language that is used conversationally or familiarly—e.g., "What's up?"—in contrast to formal, professional, or academic language—"How are you this evening?"

Vernacular refers to the native, everyday language of a place. Historically, for instance, Bibles and religious services across Europe were primarily offered in Latin, even centuries after the fall of the Roman Empire. After the revolution of the printing press and the widespread availability of vernacular translations of the Bible in the fifteenth and sixteenth centuries, everyday citizens were able to study from Bibles in their own language without needing specialized training in Latin.

A *regionalism* is a word or expression used in a particular region. In the United States, for instance, examples of regionalisms might be *soda*, *pop*, or *Coke*—terms that vary in popularity according to region.

Jargon is vocabulary used within a specialized field, such as computer programming or mechanics. Jargon may consist of specialized words or of everyday words that have a different meaning in this specialized context.

Slang refers to non-standard expressions that are not used in elevated speech and writing. Slang creates linguistic in-groups and out-groups of people, those who can understand the slang terms and those who can't. Slang is often tied to a specific time period. For example, "groovy" and "far out" are connected to the 1970s, and "as if!" and "4-1-1-" are connected to the 1990s.

A language arts classroom should demonstrate the history and evolution of language, rather than presenting fixed, unchangeable linguistic regulations. Particularly for students who feel intimidated or excluded by Standard English, instructors can make lessons more relatable or inclusive by allowing students to share or explore their own patterns of language. Students can be encouraged to act as linguists or anthropologists by getting involved in projects. Some examples include asking them to identify and compare slang in their generation to slang from their parents' generation, to exchange information about their dialect with students who come from different cultural backgrounds, or to conduct a linguistic survey of their friends, family, or neighbors. Language arts class can also be integrated with history topics by having students research unfamiliar slang or words that have shifted in meaning from the past until now—a type of study particularly useful when reading a text from a past era.

Understanding Dialect and its Appropriateness

While students should come away from class feeling supported in their linguistic diversity, the reality is that certain forms of language are viewed differently depending on the context. Lessons learned in the classroom have a real-life application to a student's future, so he or she should know where, when, and how to utilize different forms of language.

For students preparing for college, knowledge of the conventions of Standard English is essential. The same is true for students who plan to enter professional job fields. Without necessarily having a word for it, many students are already familiar with the concept of *code-switching*—altering speech patterns depending upon context. For example, a person might use a different accent or slang with neighborhood friends than with coworkers or pick up new vocabulary and speech patterns after moving to a new region, either unconsciously or consciously. In this way, speakers have an innate understanding of how their language use helps them fit into any given situation.

Instructors can design activities that help students pay attention to their language use in a given context. When discussing a novel in class, students might be encouraged to spend a few minutes freewriting in a journal to generate ideas and express their unedited thoughts. Later, though, students will then be asked to present those thoughts in a formal writing assignment that requires adherence to Standard English grammar, employing academic vocabulary and expressions appropriate to literary discussions. Alternatively, students might design an advertisement that appeals to teenagers and another one that appeals to adults, utilizing different language in each. In this way, students can learn how to reformulate their thoughts using the language appropriate to the task at hand.

Awareness of dialect can also help students as readers, too. Many writers of literary fiction and nonfiction utilize dialect and colloquialisms to add verisimilitude to their writing. This is especially true for authors who focus on a particular region or cultural group in their works, also known as *regionalism* or *local color literature*. Examples include Zora Neale Hurston's *Their Eyes Were Watching God* and the short stories of Kate Chopin. Students can be asked to consider how the speech patterns in a text affect a reader's understanding of the characters—how the pattern reflects a character's background and place in society. They might consider a reader's impression of the region—how similar or different it is from the reader's region or what can be inferred about the region based on how people speak. In some

cases, unfamiliar dialect may be very difficult for readers to understand on the page but becomes much more intelligible when read aloud—as in the reading of Shakespeare.

Reading passages together in class and then finding recordings or videos of the dialect presented in the text can help familiarize students with different speech patterns. And of course, students should also consider how use of dialect affects the audience or if it is directed to a specific audience. Who was the intended audience for *Their Eyes Were Watching God*, a novel that recreates the speech patterns of African Americans in early 1900s Florida? How might the novel be understood differently by readers who recognize that dialect than by readers who are encountering it for the first time? What would be lost if the characters didn't converse in their local dialect? Being alert to these questions creates students who are attuned to the nuances of language use in everyday life.

Identifying Research-Based Approaches for Diverse Learners

Commonly Used Research-Based Strategies

For the vast majority of people, native language acquisition comes about naturally in childhood. From the time they are born, babies are usually surrounded by the language use of their parents or caregivers. The human brain is hardwired to learn language, meaning that babies do not have to put conscious effort into unraveling the intricacies of grammar or pronunciation; it is something that happens automatically as they are exposed to language. Furthermore, caregivers do not have to formally teach first language skills to babies.

First language acquisition in infancy and early childhood passes through several predictable stages. Babies begin by crying to express a range of emotions like hunger or discomfort. By the time they are two months old, they then begin cooing to convey other emotions, such as happiness and satisfaction. In later months, infants start to experiment with different sounds like babbling and gurgling by repeating simple syllables like "goo goo goo" and "ma ma ma" and show signs of comprehending certain full words. A baby's first word often occurs around one year of age, and for the next six months, the baby can conduct simple communication through one-word expressions like "Daddy," "milk," and "cat."

After they reach eighteen months, young children begin to use two- and three-word utterances to express more complex meaning, such as "Mommy go?" "Don't want to!" and "Where juice?" By the time they are two and a half years old, toddlers enter the telegraphic stage of language where they begin using the grammatical structure of their native language, although not without some problems. A common error is "I goed to school," instead of "I went to school." However, even though young children do make mistakes in their language usage, it is nevertheless remarkable that they achieve functional mastery of a language in such a short amount of time, generally without any formal instruction.

Although acquisition of a first language is largely a natural process of childhood development, *second language acquisition* in older children or adults is quite different. This is partially linked to the critical period hypothesis, which states that language acquisition only occurs readily and naturally during the first few years of life; language acquisition that happens later, perhaps after puberty, is much more difficult and less successful. Children who are not exposed to any language before the age of five or so will have extreme difficulty learning a language later. This seems to indicate that the brain is primed to learn language from birth, but this readiness quickly diminishes after the critical period has been passed.

Although scientists continue to debate the exact significance of a critical period on second language development, learning a second language later in life clearly presents different challenges than learning a first language. In linguistics, **L1** refers to a speaker's native language and **L2** refers to a second language.

L2 acquisition follows different stages from that of L1. L2 acquisition begins with *preproduction*, also known as the *silent stage*, during which the learner is exposed to the new language, but lacks the skills to communicate and may only use body language or other non-verbal expressions. During the early production stage, the L2 learner begins using simple expressions and has limited comprehension ability.

Next is *speech emergence*—the low-intermediate stage. At this point, the language learner can form simple sentences although he or she makes frequent errors in grammar and usage. L2 learners then pass to *intermediate fluency*, where they begin to gain skills in academic or idiomatic language, demonstrate a much higher level of comprehension, and make fewer mistakes in their expressions.

Finally, the learner reaches *advanced fluency*, exhibiting near-native expressive and comprehensive skills. It is worth noting that even with near-native skills, after many years of advanced fluency, L2 learners may continue to speak with a different accent or use certain idiosyncratic expressions that are markedly different from native speakers. Nevertheless, they are certainly fluent.

In 2013, the Census Bureau reported that one in five Americans are speaking a language other than English at home, so language arts instructors will encounter a mixture of native speakers and second language learners in the classroom. In both cases, though, certain goals and strategies remain the same. The purpose of a language arts class is not to teach students language from scratch, but rather to further develop their preexisting knowledge and increase their awareness of how to use language for more effective and meaningful communication.

For both native and non-native English speakers, the exposure to written and spoken language that they receive outside of school impacts their future performance in school. In a notable 1995 study, researchers observed children in low- and high-income families and found that those in high-income households were exposed to 30 million more words during their childhood than those from families on welfare. When researchers followed up on these children in third grade, those who had been exposed to more words early on showed greater success in measures of reading comprehension and vocabulary.

As the early stages of both L1 and L2 acquisition show, learners need language input before they can achieve language output. Providing students with a variety of language resources, both formally and informally, can give them valuable exposure to new means of expression. In class, this exposure can include daily assignments, a classroom library, or a bulletin board with news for students. Educators can also get students in the habit of accessing resources outside of the classroom such as visiting the school or public library, watching, reading, or listening to the news, or reading informally from magazines, blogs, or other sources of interest.

This exposure also relates to two different forms of vocabulary acquisition—through incidental learning or direct instruction. *Incidental learning* occurs when students naturally encounter new vocabulary in context during daily life whereas *direct instruction* occurs through structured lessons and assignments in an academic setting.

In vocabulary development in particular, when it comes to direct instruction, there are several approaches to teaching new words to students.

One is the *three-tier approach*, which states that vocabulary can be classified into three levels as shown in the graphic below.

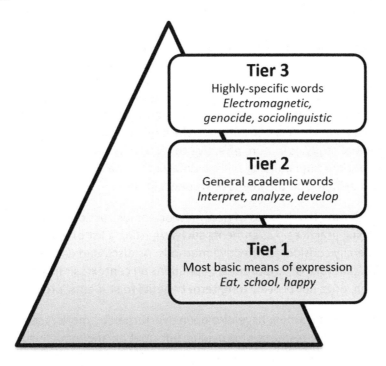

Tier three words should be taught within the subjects that they are directly related to rather than in a language arts class. Instead, language arts instruction should focus on tier two words that are broadly applicable to a range of subjects and, therefore, more practical for students.

Another theory of vocabulary development is learning language through chunks or groups of related words. By learning words in context along with other connected words, students are better able to connect vocabulary to areas of prior knowledge and more effectively store new words in their long-term memory. Students also gain a more complete set of tools with which to form new expressions, rather than simply learning new words in isolation. Learning in *semantic chunks*—clusters of five to ten words forming a connected phrase or sentence—is particularly useful for L2 learners in gaining familiarity with how to manipulate vocabulary and combine words to build meaning.

Vocabulary learning can also be conducted through a variety of media, combining visual, auditory, and active cues. One strategy is known as the *total physical response*, where students learn to associate a word with a certain physical reaction. For example, in response to the word *circumference*, students might use their finger to draw a circle in the air. Students can also watch videos related to the vocabulary topic they are learning about or look at visual representations of new words through a picture dictionary. By activating different styles of learning, instructors can provide students with more opportunities to acquire new language skills.

Evaluating the Effectiveness of Specific Strategies
New research on teaching strategies is emerging all the time, and it is important for instructors to stay abreast of new developments while evaluating when and how to implement any changes in their classroom. Instructors should also consider the pros and cons of different approaches to teaching.

In terms of encouraging students to seek outside language resources (noted the section above), the effectiveness differs greatly depending on students' background and home life. Students who must work after school to support themselves or their families may not have much time to stop by the public library or to read for leisure; in this case, instructors need to maximize in-class instruction time. According to another strategy, the three-tier approach, tier two words are most important in a language arts classroom. However, some L2 students in the early production or intermediate fluency stages may lack basic tier one skills and struggle with understanding more advanced academic vocabulary.

Also, the integrated approach to learning vocabulary in a group of related words calls on instructors to present words as they are actually used in context, which might involve using some tier three words related to specific fields of study. Is it more effective to focus only on having a broad base of general vocabulary or to spend some time building skills in different specialized areas? This question might be answered differently depending on the needs of students in class.

As they experiment with the effectiveness of new methods of instruction, educators can also move beyond outdated learning practices. Assignments such as getting a list of words to look up in the dictionary are not generally considered effective methods. As discussed earlier, words contain a multitude of meanings that take on importance dependent on context; simply memorizing words outside of context, then, does not provide long-term benefits to students' productive language skills.

Instructor-centered models of learning have also been overturned by more recent pedagogical research. While instructors are a valuable resource of providing information and modeling language use for students, educators simply supply the input while students still need a chance to produce output. This means giving students ample opportunity to practice and apply new vocabulary, calling on students' prior knowledge when introducing new vocabulary, and demonstrating how students can use language skills outside of the classroom.

Interpreting Research and Applying it to Language Challenges

For instructors, pedagogical research is only as valuable as its real-life application in the classroom. Educators need to be able to use research-based strategies to tackle issues that arise while teaching.

One challenge may be the gap that exists between students who come to class with a high degree of literacy and language skills and students who have had fewer opportunities to develop those skills before entering the classroom. For example, some students have no access to a computer or the Internet at home or have a limited/nonexistent home library. Closing the gap through basic media literacy—perhaps in collaboration with a school media specialist—can empower students to know how to access language resources through the library, Internet, or other sources and how to utilize these resources for both learning and leisure. The concept of vocabulary development through incidental learning holds that students will benefit from any reading material, so instructors can encourage students to pursue their own interests through reading if they seem disinterested in textbook offerings. Asking students to keep a personal reading log or daily journal can encourage them to make reading and writing part of their everyday lives.

Another common problem in language instruction is students forgetting new vocabulary as soon as they learn it. Repetition and reinforcement is key to creating lasting knowledge. Also, as many studies point to the importance of learning vocabulary in context, utilizing contextual learning strategies can help students build onto prior knowledge rather than treat every new word as something strange and unfamiliar. This can be done by prompting students for what they already know when a new concept is introduced in class, introduce possible unfamiliar words that they might encounter in a text, and

encourage them to use context clues as they read to make logical guesses about how unknown words are connected to known ones. These strategies further empower learners to utilize the knowledge that they already possess.

Incorporating multimedia resources can also be a powerful tool for providing meaningful instruction for students with a variety of learning styles. If students struggle to remember new vocabulary words, strategies such as total physical response or recognizing a picture associated with the word can provide students with different tools to secure information in their long-term memory.

In terms of research specific to L2 learning, knowledge of the stages of development can help instructors handle frustrations that may arise during second language learning. For example, teachers may worry that students understand nothing during the silent period, but students are absorbing the basic linguistic information that they will need to start forming utterances. Rather than giving up and getting discouraged from the start, instructors can continue providing basic communication information that students will be ready to use within the first few weeks or months of being exposed to a new language.

Practice Questions

1. What is the structure of the following sentence?

    The restaurant is unconventional because it serves both Chicago style pizza and New York style pizza.

    a. Simple
    b. Compound
    c. Complex
    d. Compound-complex

2. The following sentence contains what kind of error?

    This summer, I'm planning to travel to Italy, take a Mediterranean cruise, going to Pompeii, and eat a lot of Italian food.

    a. Parallelism
    b. Sentence fragment
    c. Misplaced modifier
    d. Subject-verb agreement

3. The following sentence contains what kind of error?

    Forgetting that he was supposed to meet his girlfriend for dinner, Anita was mad when Fred showed up late.

    a. Parallelism
    b. Run-on sentence
    c. Misplaced modifier
    d. Subject-verb agreement

4. The following sentence contains what kind of error?

    Some workers use all their sick leave, other workers cash out their leave.

    a. Parallelism
    b. Comma splice
    c. Sentence fragment
    d. Subject-verb agreement

5. A student writes the following in an essay:

    Protestors filled the streets of the city. Because they were dissatisfied with the government's leadership.

Which of the following is an appropriately-punctuated correction for this sentence?

    a. Protestors filled the streets of the city, because they were dissatisfied with the government's leadership.
    b. Protesters, filled the streets of the city, because they were dissatisfied with the government's leadership.
    c. Because they were dissatisfied with the government's leadership protestors filled the streets of the city.
    d. Protestors filled the streets of the city because they were dissatisfied with the government's leadership.

6. What is the part of speech of the underlined word in the sentence?

    We need to come up with a fresh <u>approach</u> to this problem.

    a. Noun
    b. Verb
    c. Adverb
    d. Adjective

7. What is the part of speech of the underlined word in the sentence?

    Investigators conducted an <u>exhaustive</u> inquiry into the accusations of corruption.

    a. Noun
    b. Verb
    c. Adverb
    d. Adjective

8. The underlined portion of the sentence is an example of which sentence component?

    New students should report <u>to the student center</u>.

    a. Dependent clause
    b. Adverbial phrase
    c. Adjective clause
    d. Noun phrase

9. What is the noun phrase in the following sentence?

    Charlotte's new German shepherd puppy is energetic.

    a. Puppy
    b. Charlotte
    c. German shepherd puppy
    d. Charlotte's new German shepherd puppy

10. Which word choices will correctly complete the sentence?

Increasing the price of bus fares has had a greater [affect / effect] on ridership [then / than] expected.

a. affect; then
b. affect; than
c. effect; then
d. effect; than

11. While studying vocabulary, a student notices that the words *circumference*, *circumnavigate*, and *circumstance* all begin with the prefix *circum–*. The student uses her knowledge of affixes to infer that all of these words share what related meaning?

a. Around, surrounding
b. Travel, transport
c. Size, measurement
d. Area, location

12. A student wants to rewrite the following sentence:

Entrepreneurs use their ideas to make money.

He wants to use the word *money* as a verb, but he isn't sure which word ending to use. What is the appropriate suffix to add to *money* to complete the following sentence?

Entrepreneurs _____ their ideas.

a. –ize
b. –ical
c. –en
d. –ful

13. A student reads the following sentence:

A hundred years ago, automobiles were rare, but now cars are ubiquitous.

However, she doesn't know what the word *ubiquitous* means. Which key context clue is essential to decipher the word's meaning?

a. Ago
b. Cars
c. Now
d. Rare

14. A local newspaper is looking for writers for a student column. A student would like to submit his article to the newspaper, but he isn't sure how to format his article according to journalistic standards. What resource should he use?

a. A thesaurus
b. A dictionary
c. A style guide
d. A grammar book

15. A student encounters the word *aficionado* and wants to learn more about it. It doesn't sound like other English words he knows, so the student is curious to identify the word's origin. What resource should he consult?
    a. A thesaurus
    b. A dictionary
    c. A style guide
    d. A grammar book

16. Which domain is likely to be used by a website run by a nonprofit group?
    a. .com
    b. .edu
    c. .org
    d. .gov

17. Several generations ago, immigrants and locals in a region developed a simplified mixture of their two languages in order to carry out basic communication tasks. However, usage of this mixed language increased, and later generations passed it down to their children as their first language. These children are now speaking what kind of language?
    a. A pidgin
    b. A Creole
    c. A jargon
    d. A regionalism

18. Which of the following is true of Standard English?
    a. It is one dialect of English.
    b. It is the original form of English.
    c. It is the most complex form of English.
    d. It is the form that follows grammatical rules.

19. A teacher notices that, when students are talking to each other between classes, they are using their own unique vocabulary words and expressions to talk about their daily lives. When the teacher hears these non-standard words that are specific to one age or cultural group, what type of language is she listening to?
    a. Slang
    b. Jargon
    c. Dialect
    d. Vernacular

20. A teacher wants to counsel a student about using the word *ain't* in a research paper for a high school English class. What advice should the teacher give?
    a. *Ain't* is not in the dictionary, so it isn't a word.
    b. Because the student isn't in college yet, *ain't* is an appropriate expression for a high school writer.
    c. *Ain't* is incorrect English and should not be part of a serious student's vocabulary because it sounds uneducated.
    d. *Ain't* is a colloquial expression, and while it may be appropriate in a conversational setting, it is not standard in academic writing.

21. Which of the following is true of first language acquisition?
    a. Children need some instruction from parents or caregivers to learn a first language.
    b. Children first begin forming complete words when they are about two years old.
    c. Children experiment with the sounds of a language before they form words.
    d. Children have no language comprehension before they can speak.

22. Which of the following is true of second language acquisition?
    a. Students learn best through memorization of new vocabulary words.
    b. Second language acquisition follows the same stages as first language acquisition.
    c. Advanced fluency is achieved when the speaker has no accent in his or her second language.
    d. Second language learners experience a preproduction stage, during which they are unable to produce verbal expressions.

23. Which of the following would NOT be a recommended vocabulary teaching strategy?
    a. Focusing on specialized academic jargon that students will encounter in college
    b. Creating a word map to understand the connection between vocabulary terms
    c. Accessing prior knowledge when introducing a new area of vocabulary
    d. Providing examples of how to use terms inside and outside of class

24. Which of the following is an example of incidental learning in vocabulary development?
    a. After reading a story in class, the teacher provides students with a list of keywords to know from the text.
    b. While reading a novel for class, a student encounters an unfamiliar word and looks it up in the dictionary.
    c. As part of a writing assignment, students are instructed to utilize certain academic words and expressions in their essay.
    d. After getting back the results of a vocabulary exam, students are assigned to make personal study guides based on the words that they missed on the test.

25. A teacher is considering integrating some media sources like television and the Internet into his classroom, but he is unsure of how effective it will be. Which of the following is true about media literacy in language development?
    a. Instruction should focus only on professional media sources such as scientific journals and mainstream news publications to emphasize Standard English skills.
    b. In the twenty-first century, every student has access to and proficiency in using the Internet, so it is unnecessary to spend time on building skills in class.
    c. Students should explore media resources in their personal areas of interest to develop regular language habits in an enjoyable way.
    d. The Internet serves as a huge distraction for students and should not be part of instruction.

Answer Explanations

1. C: A complex sentence joins an independent or main clause with a dependent or subordinate clause. In this case, the main clause is "The restaurant is unconventional." This is a clause with one subject-verb combination that can stand alone as a grammatically-complete sentence. The dependent clause is "because it serves both Chicago style pizza and New York style pizza." This clause begins with the subordinating conjunction *because* and also consists of only one subject-verb combination. *A* is incorrect because a simple sentence consists of only one verb-subject combination—one independent clause. *B* is incorrect because a compound sentence contains two independent clauses connected by a conjunction. *D* is incorrect because a complex-compound sentence consists of two or more independent clauses and one or more dependent clauses.

2. A: Parallelism refers to consistent use of sentence structure or word form. In this case, the list within the sentence does not utilize parallelism; three of the verbs appear in their base form—*travel*, *take*, and *eat*—but one appears as a gerund—*going*. A parallel version of this sentence would be "This summer, I'm planning to travel to Italy, take a Mediterranean cruise, go to Pompeii, and eat a lot of Italian food." *B* is incorrect because this description is a complete sentence. *C* is incorrect as a misplaced modifier is a modifier that is not located appropriately in relation to the word or words they modify. *D* is incorrect because subject-verb agreement refers to the appropriate conjugation of a verb in relation to its subject.

3. C: In this sentence, the modifier is the phrase "Forgetting that he was supposed to meet his girlfriend for dinner." This phrase offers information about Fred's actions, but the noun that immediately follows it is Anita, creating some confusion about the "do-er" of the phrase. A more appropriate sentence arrangement would be "Forgetting that he was supposed to meet his girlfriend for dinner, Fred made Anita mad when he showed up late." *A* is incorrect as parallelism refers to the consistent use of sentence structure and verb tense, and this sentence is appropriately consistent. *B* is incorrect as a run-on sentence does not contain appropriate punctuation for the number of independent clauses presented, which is not true of this description. *D* is incorrect because subject-verb agreement refers to the appropriate conjugation of a verb relative to the subject, and all verbs have been properly conjugated.

4. B: A comma splice occurs when a comma is used to join two independent clauses together without the additional use of an appropriate conjunction. One way to remedy this problem is to replace the comma with a semicolon. Another solution is to add a conjunction: "Some workers use all their sick leave, but other workers cash out their leave." *A* is incorrect as parallelism refers to the consistent use of sentence structure and verb tense; all tenses and structures in this sentence are consistent. *C* is incorrect because a sentence fragment is a phrase or clause that cannot stand alone—this sentence contains two independent clauses. *D* is incorrect because subject-verb agreement refers to the proper conjugation of a verb relative to the subject, and all verbs have been properly conjugated.

5. D: The problem in the original passage is that the second sentence is a dependent clause that cannot stand alone as a sentence; it must be attached to the main clause found in the first sentence. Because the main clause comes first, it does not need to be separated by a comma. However, if the dependent clause came first, then a comma would be necessary, which is why Choice *C* is incorrect. *A* and *B* also insert unnecessary commas into the sentence.

6. A: A noun refers to a person, place, thing, or idea. Although the word *approach* can also be used as a verb, in the sentence it functions as a noun within the noun phrase "a fresh approach," so *B* is incorrect. An adverb is a word or phrase that provides additional information of the verb, but because the verb is *need* and not *approach*, then *C* is false. An adjective is a word that describes a noun, used here as the word *fresh*, but it is not the noun itself. Thus, *D* is also incorrect.

7. D: An adjective modifies a noun, answering the question "Which one?" or "What kind?" In this sentence, the word *exhaustive* is an adjective that modifies the noun *investigation*. Another clue that this word is an adjective is the suffix *–ive*, which means "having the quality of." The nouns in this sentence are investigators, inquiry, accusations, and corruption; therefore, A is incorrect. The verb in this sentence is *conducted* because this was the action taken by the subject *the investigators*; therefore, *B* is incorrect. *C* is incorrect because an adverb is a word or phrase that provides additional information about the verb, expressing how, when, where, or in what manner.

8. B: In this case, the phrase functions as an adverb modifying the verb *report*, so *B* is the correct answer. "To the student center" does not consist of a subject-verb combination, so it is not a clause; thus, Choices *A* and *C* can be eliminated. This group of words is a phrase. Phrases are classified by either the controlling word in the phrase or its function in the sentence. *D* is incorrect because a noun phrase is a series of words that describe or modify a noun.

9. D: A noun phrase consists of the noun and all of its modifiers. In this case, the subject of the sentence is the noun *puppy*, but it is preceded by several modifiers—adjectives that give more information about what kind of puppy, which are also part of the noun phrase. Thus, *A* is incorrect. Charlotte is the owner of the puppy and a modifier of the puppy, so *B* is false. *C* is incorrect because it contains some, but not all, of the modifiers pertaining to the puppy. *D* is correct because it contains all of them.

10. D: In this sentence, the first answer choice requires a noun meaning *impact* or *influence*, so *effect* is the correct answer. For the second answer choice, the sentence is drawing a comparison. *Than* shows a comparative relationship whereas *then* shows sequence or consequence. *A* and *C* can be eliminated because they contain the choice *then*. *B* is incorrect because *affect* is a verb while this sentence requires a noun.

11. A: The affix *circum–* originates from Latin and means *around or surrounding*. It is also related to other round words, such as circle and circus. The rest of the choices do not relate to the affix *circum–* and are therefore incorrect.

12. A: Only two of these suffixes, *–ize* and *–en*, can be used to form verbs, so *B* and *D* are incorrect. Those choices create adjectives. The suffix *–ize* means "to convert or turn into." The suffix *–en* means "to become." Because this sentence is about converting ideas into money, money + *–ize* or *monetize* is the most appropriate word to complete the sentence, so *C* is incorrect.

13. D: Students can use context clues to make a careful guess about the meaning of unfamiliar words. Although all of the words in a sentence can help contribute to the overall sentence, in this case, the adjective that pairs with *ubiquitous* gives the most important hint to the student—cars were first *rare*, but now they are *ubiquitous*. The inversion of *rare* is what gives meaning to the rest of the sentence and *ubiquitous* means "existing everywhere" or "not rare." *A* is incorrect because *ago* only indicates a time frame. *B* is incorrect because *cars* does not indicate a contrasting relationship to the word *ubiquitous* to provide a good context clue. *C* is incorrect because it also only indicates a time frame, but used together with *rare*, it provides the contrasting relationship needed to identify the meaning of the unknown word.

14. C: A style guide offers advice about proper formatting, punctuation, and usage when writing for a specific field, such as journalism or scientific research. The other resources would not offer similar information. A dictionary is useful for looking up definitions; a thesaurus is useful for looking up synonyms and antonyms. A grammar book is useful for looking up specific grammar topics. Thus, Choices *A*, *C*, and *D* are incorrect.

15. B: A word's origin is also known as its *etymology*. In addition to offering a detailed list of a word's various meanings, a dictionary also provides information about a word's history, such as when it first came into use, what language it originated from, and how its meaning may have changed over time. A thesaurus is for identifying synonyms and antonyms, so *A* is incorrect. A style guide provides formatting, punctuation, and syntactical advice for a specific field, and a grammar book is related to the appropriate placement of words and punctuation, which does not provide any insight into a word's meaning. Therefore, Choices *A*, *C*, and *D* are incorrect.

16. C: The .org domain on websites is generally used by nonprofit groups or community organizations. A government website uses .gov, and .edu is used for educational institutions. Private companies and businesses use .com, so Choices *A*, *B*, and *D* are incorrect.

17. B: A utilitarian combination of two or more languages that springs up where different linguistic groups overlap is known as a pidgin; it is used for communication tasks but not as a first language. However, when that pidgin becomes entrenched in the culture and is then taught to children as their first, native language, it is known as a Creole. *C* and *D* are not correct because they both refer to vocabulary, not to entire languages. Jargon is the vocabulary of a specific field or industry, and regionalisms are the vocabulary of a specific place.

18. A: A dialect of a language refers to one version of that language that follows specific patterns of grammar, spelling, pronunciation, and vocabulary. In this sense, then, Standard English is simply one of many different dialects of English. Standard English is not the original form of English because the language has evolved considerably over the past several centuries and will most likely continue to do so in the future. Also, there is nothing that makes Standard English more complex or grammatical than other dialects of English. Although other dialects may deviate from the grammar used in Standard English, these dialects still follow their own predictable rules and patterns of grammar.

19. A: Slang refers to non-standard expressions that are not used in elevated speech and writing. Slang tends to be specific to one group or time period and is commonly used within groups of young people during their conversations with each other. Jargon refers to the language used in a specialized field. The vernacular is the native language of a local area, and a dialect is one form of a language in a certain region. Thus, *B*, *C*, and *D* are incorrect.

20. D: Colloquial language is that which is used conversationally or informally, in contrast to professional or academic language. While *ain't* is common in conversational English, it is a non-standard expression in academic writing. For college-bound students, high school should introduce them to the expectations of a college classroom, so *B* is not the best answer. Teachers should also avoid placing moral or social value on certain patterns of speech. Rather than teaching students that their familiar speech patterns are bad, teachers should help students learn when and how to use appropriate forms of expression, so *C* is wrong. *Ain't* is in the dictionary, so *A* is incorrect, both in the reason for counseling and in the factual sense.

21. C: In the babbling stage, children repeat simple syllables that will later form the building blocks of their first words, such as ma-ma and da-da. *A* is not a correct answer because children learn their first language simply by being exposed to it, without any formal instruction required. *B* is also incorrect because most children utter their first word by about one year old. Babies demonstrate understanding of language before they are able to actually form words themselves, so *D* is not correct.

22. D: This is the first stage of L2 acquisition, before the learner is ready to communicate in the target language. Both L1 and L2 acquisition clearly follow different stages, so *B* is incorrect. The final stage of L2 development, advanced fluency, does not require the speaker to have a native accent; rather, it refers to the stage at which the speaker encounters no difficulty in expression or comprehension in both conversational and academic settings; thus, *C* is incorrect. L2 learners benefit from a variety of instruction techniques, and students require both input—such as studying new vocabulary words—and output—actually using those words in productive language tasks—in order to develop new skills; therefore, *A* is also incorrect.

23. A: Although it is useful to introduce students to concepts they might encounter in a college classroom, making jargon the focus of instruction at the expense of vocabulary with more widely-applicable usage will not meet the needs of the majority of students in class. The other strategies are all appropriate ways to have students integrate new vocabulary into their existing knowledge structures and their everyday lives.

24. B: Incidental learning contrasts with direct instruction, wherein instructors direct students in the precise meaning of new vocabulary or call students' attention to important vocabulary skills in a given lesson. In incidental learning, students learn new vocabulary as they encounter unfamiliar terms during other learning tasks. In this case, *B* is the correct answer because the student uses a reading assignment as an opportunity to learn a new word. In all of the other answer choices, the instructor is the one guiding the students' attention towards specific vocabulary words.

25. C: Students should explore media resources in their personal areas of interest to develop regular language habits in an enjoyable way. Multimedia resources are a powerful educational resource and should be integrated into class instruction when possible, making *D* a poor answer choice. *B* is incorrect because it cannot be assumed that every student has regular access to the internet, and even students who do have home internet access may still need guidance in how to use it to find learning resources. *A* is incorrect because though it is useful to introduce students to academic and professional media sources, the diversity of media available means that these do not need to be the sole emphasis of instruction. Rather, it can be useful to help students explore areas of their own interest and build skills in how to apply language development concepts—e.g., reading comprehension skills, using context to learn new words, keeping a journal of new words and expressions, or formulating a reading response—both inside and outside of the classroom.

Writing, Speaking, and Listening

Identifying Modes of Writing

Distinguishing Between Common Modes of Writing

To distinguish between the common modes of writing, it is important to identify the primary purpose of the work. This can be determined by considering what the author is trying to say to the reader. Although there are countless different styles of writing, all written works tend to fall under four primary categories: argumentative/persuasive, informative expository, descriptive, and narrative.

The below table highlights the purpose, distinct characteristics, and examples of each rhetorical mode.

Writing Mode	Purpose	Distinct Characteristics	Examples
Argumentative	To persuade	Opinions, loaded or subjective language, evidence, suggestions of what the reader should do, calls to action	Critical reviews Political journals Letters of recommendation Cover letters Advertising
Informative	To teach or inform	Objective language, definitions, instructions, factual information	Business and scientific reports Textbooks Instruction manuals News articles Personal letters Wills Informative essays Travel guides Study guides
Descriptive	To deliver sensory details to the reader	Heavy use of adjectives and imagery, language that appeals to any of the five senses	Poetry Journal entries Often used in narrative mode
Narrative	To tell a story, share an experience, entertain	Series of events, plot, characters, dialogue, conflict	Novels Short stories Novellas Anecdotes Biographies Epic poems Autobiographies

Identifying Common Types of Writing

The following steps help to identify examples of common types within the modes of writing:

1. Identifying the audience—to whom or for whom the author is writing
2. Determining the author's purpose—why the author is writing the piece
3. Analyzing the word choices and how they are used

To demonstrate, the following passage has been marked to illustrate *the addressee*, the author's purpose, and word choices:

> *To Whom It May Concern*:
>
> I am <u>extraordinarily excited</u> to be applying to the Master of Environmental Science program at Australian National University. I believe the richness in biological and cultural diversity, as well as Australia's close proximity to the Great Barrier Reef, would provide a <u>deeply fulfilling</u> educational experience. *I am writing to express why I believe I would be an <u>excellent</u> addition to the program.*
>
> While in college, I participated in a three-month public health internship in Ecuador, where I spent time both learning about medicine in a third world country and also about the Ecuadorian environment, including the Amazon Jungle and the Galápagos Islands. <u>My favorite experience</u> through the internship, besides swimming with sea lions in San Cristóbal, was helping to neutralize parasitic potable water and collect samples for analysis in Puyo.
>
> Though my undergraduate studies related primarily to the human body, I took several courses in natural science, including a year of chemistry, biology, and physics as well as a course in a calculus. <u>I am confident</u> that my fundamental knowledge in these fields will prepare me for the science courses integral to the Masters of Environmental Science.

Having identified the *addressee*, it is evident that this selection is a letter of some kind. Further inspection into the author's purpose, seen in *bold*, shows that the author is trying to explain why he or she should be accepted into the environmental science program, which automatically places it into the argumentative mode as the writer is trying to persuade the reader to agree and to incite the reader into action by encouraging the program to accept the writer as a candidate. In addition to revealing the purpose, the use of emotional language—extraordinarily, excellent, deeply fulfilling, favorite experience, confident—illustrates that this is a persuasive piece. It also provides evidence for why this person would be an excellent addition to the program—his/her experience in Ecuador and with scientific curriculum.

The following passage presents an opportunity to solidify this method of analysis and practice the steps above to determine the mode of writing:

> The biological effects of laughter have long been an interest of medicine and psychology. Laughing is often speculated to reduce blood pressure because it induces feelings of relaxation and elation. Participating students watched a series of videos that elicited laughter, and their blood pressure was taken before and after the viewings. An average decrease in blood pressure was observed, though resulting p-values attest that the results were not significant.

This selection contains factual and scientific information, is devoid of any adjectives or flowery descriptions, and is not trying to convince the reader of any particular stance. Though the audience is

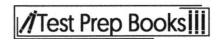

not directly addressed, the purpose of the passage is to present the results of an experiment to those who would be interested in the biological effects of laughter—most likely a scientific community. Thus, this passage is an example of informative writing.

Below is another passage to help identify examples of the common writing modes, taken from *The Endeavor Journal of Sir Joseph Banks*:

10th May 1769 – THE ENGLISH CREW GET TAHITIAN NAMES

We have now got the Indian name of the Island, Otahite, so therefore for the future I shall call it. As for our own names the Indians find so much dificulty in pronouncing them that we are forcd to indulge them in calling us what they please, or rather what they say when they attempt to pronounce them. I give here the List: Captn Cooke *Toote*, Dr Solander *Torano*, Mr Hicks *Hete*, Mr Gore *Toárro*, Mr Molineux *Boba* from his Christian name Robert, Mr Monkhouse *Mato*, and myself *Tapáne*. In this manner they have names for almost every man in the ship.

This extract contains no elements of an informative or persuasive intent and does not seem to follow any particular line of narrative. The passage gives a list of the different names that the Indians have given the crew members, as well as the name of an island. Although there is no context for the selection, through the descriptions, it is clear that the author and his comrades are on an island trying to communicate with the native inhabitants. Hence, this passage is a journal that reflects the descriptive mode.

These are only a few of the many examples that can be found in the four primary modes of writing.

Determining the Appropriate Mode of Writing

The author's *primary purpose* is defined as the reason an author chooses to write a selection, and it is often dependent on his or her *audience*. A biologist writing a textbook, for example, does so to communicate scientific knowledge to an audience of people who want to study biology. An audience can be as broad as the entire global population or as specific as women fighting for equal rights in the bicycle repair industry. Whatever the audience, it is important that the author considers its demographics—age, gender, culture, language, education level, etc.

If the author's purpose is to persuade or inform, he or she will consider how much the intended audience knows about the subject. For example, if an author is writing on the importance of recycling to anyone who will listen, he or she will use the informative mode—including background information on recycling—and the argumentative mode—evidence for why it works, while also using simple diction so that it is easy for everyone to understand. If, on the other hand, the writer is proposing new methods for recycling using solar energy, the audience is probably already familiar with standard recycling processes and will require less background information, as well as more technical language inherent to the scientific community.

If the author's purpose is to entertain through a story or a poem, he or she will need to consider whom he/she is trying to entertain. If an author is writing a script for a children's cartoon, the plot, language, conflict, characters, and humor would align with the interests of the age demographic of that audience. On the other hand, if an author is trying to entertain adults, he or she may write content not suitable for children. The author's purpose and audience are generally interdependent.

Understanding the Task, Purpose, and Audience

Identifying the Task, Purpose, and Intended Audience

An author's *writing style*—the way in which words, grammar, punctuation, and sentence fluidity are used—is the most influential element in a piece of writing, and it is dependent on the purpose and the audience for whom it is intended. Together, a writing style and mode of writing form the foundation of a written work, and a good writer will choose the most effective mode and style to convey a message to readers.

Writers should first determine what they are trying to say and then choose the most effective mode of writing to communicate that message. Different writing modes and *word choices* will affect the tone of a piece—that is, its underlying attitude, emotion, or character. The argumentative mode may utilize words that are earnest, angry, passionate, or excited whereas an informative piece may have a sterile, germane, or enthusiastic tone. The tones found in narratives vary greatly, depending on the purpose of the writing. *Tone* will also be affected by the audience—teaching science to children or those who may be uninterested would be most effective with enthusiastic language and exclamation points whereas teaching science to college students may take on a more serious and professional tone, with fewer charged words and punctuation choices that are inherent to academia.

Sentence fluidity—whether sentences are long and rhythmic or short and succinct—also affects a piece of writing as it determines the way in which a piece is read. Children or audiences unfamiliar with a subject do better with short, succinct sentence structures as these break difficult concepts up into shorter points. A period, question mark, or exclamation point is literally a signal for the reader to stop and takes more time to process. Thus, longer, more complex sentences are more appropriate for adults or educated audiences as they can fit more information in between processing time.

The amount of *supporting detail* provided is also tailored to the audience. A text that introduces a new subject to its readers will focus more on broad ideas without going into greater detail whereas a text that focuses on a more specific subject is likely to provide greater detail about the ideas discussed.

Writing styles, like modes, are most effective when tailored to their audiences. Having awareness of an audience's demographic is one of the most crucial aspects of properly communicating an argument, a story, or a set of information.

Choosing the Most Appropriate Type of Writing

Before beginning any writing, it is imperative that a writer have a firm grasp on the message he or she wishes to convey and how he or she wants readers to be affected by the writing. For example, does the author want readers to be more informed about the subject? Does the writer want readers to agree with his or her opinion? Does the writer want readers to get caught up in an exciting narrative? The following steps are a guide to determining the appropriate type of writing for a task, purpose, and audience:

1. Identifying the purpose for writing the piece
2. Determining the audience
3. Adapting the writing mode, word choices, tone, and style to fit the audience and the purpose

It is important to distinguish between a work's purpose and its main idea. The essential difference between the two is that the *main idea* is what the author wants to communicate about the topic at hand whereas the *primary purpose* is why the author is writing in the first place. The primary purpose is

what will determine the type of writing an author will choose to utilize, not the main idea, though the two are related. For example, if an author writes an article on the mistreatment of animals in factory farms and, at the end, suggests that people should convert to vegetarianism, the main idea is that vegetarianism would reduce the poor treatment of animals. The primary purpose is to convince the reader to stop eating animals. Since the primary purpose is to galvanize an audience into action, the author would choose the argumentative writing mode.

The next step is to consider to whom the author is appealing as this will determine the type of details to be included, the diction to be used, the tone to be employed, and the sentence structure to be used. An audience can be identified by considering the following questions:

- What is the purpose for writing the piece?
- To whom is it being written?
- What is their age range?
- Are they familiar with the material being presented, or are they just being newly introduced to it?
- Where are they from?
- Is the task at hand in a professional or casual setting?
- Is the task at hand for monetary gain?

These are just a few of the numerous considerations to keep in mind, but the main idea is to become as familiar with the audience as possible. Once the audience has been understood, the author can then adapt the writing style to align with the readers' education and interests. The audience is what determines the *rhetorical appeal* the author will use—ethos, pathos, or logos. *Ethos* is a rhetorical appeal to an audience's ethics and/or morals. Ethos is most often used in argumentative and informative writing modes. *Pathos* is an appeal to the audience's emotions and sympathies, and it is found in argumentative, descriptive, and narrative writing modes. *Logos* is an appeal to the audience's logic and reason and is used primarily in informative texts as well as in supporting details for argumentative pieces. Rhetorical appeals are discussed in depth in the informational texts and rhetoric section of the test.

If the author is trying to encourage global conversion to vegetarianism, he or she may choose to use all three rhetorical appeals to reach varying personality types. Those who are less interested in the welfare of animals but are interested in facts and science would relate more to logos. Animal lovers would relate better to an emotional appeal. In general, the most effective works utilize all three appeals.

Finally, after determining the writing mode and rhetorical appeal, the author will consider word choice, sentence structure, and tone, depending on the purpose and audience. The author may choose words that convey sadness or anger when speaking about animal welfare if writing to persuade, or he or she will stick to dispassionate and matter-of-fact tones, if informing the public on the treatment of animals in factory farms. If the author is writing to a younger or less-educated audience, he or she may choose to shorten and simplify sentence structures and word choice. If appealing to an audience with more expert knowledge on a particular subject, writers will more likely employ a style of longer sentences and more complex vocabulary.

Depending on the task, the author may choose to use a first person, second person, or third person point of view. First person and second person perspectives are inherently more casual in tone, including the author and the reader in the rhetoric, while third person perspectives are often seen in more professional settings.

Evaluating the Effectiveness of a Piece of Writing

An effective and engaging piece of writing will cause the reader to forget about the author entirely. Readers will become so engrossed in the subject, argument, or story at hand that they will almost identify with it, readily adopting beliefs proposed by the author or accepting all elements of the story as believable. On the contrary, poorly written works will cause the reader to be hyperaware of the author, doubting the writer's knowledge of a subject or questioning the validity of a narrative. Persuasive or expository works that are poorly researched will have this effect, as well as poorly planned stories with significant plot holes. An author must consider the task, purpose, and audience to sculpt a piece of writing effectively.

When evaluating the effectiveness of a piece, the most important thing to consider is how well the purpose is conveyed to the audience through the mode, use of rhetoric, and writing style.

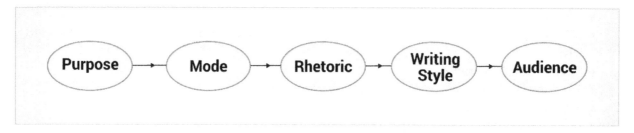

The purpose must pass through these three aspects for effective delivery to the audience. If any elements are not properly considered, the reader will be overly aware of the author, and the message will be lost. The following is a checklist for evaluating the effectiveness of a piece:

- Does the writer choose the appropriate writing mode—argumentative, narrative, descriptive, informative—for his or her purpose?
- Does the writing mode employed contain characteristics inherent to that mode?
- Does the writer consider the personalities/interests/demographics of the intended audience when choosing rhetorical appeals?
- Does the writer use appropriate vocabulary, sentence structure, voice, and tone for the audience demographic?
- Does the author properly establish himself/herself as having authority on the subject, if applicable?
- Does the piece make sense?

Another thing to consider is the medium in which the piece was written. If the medium is a blog, diary, or personal letter, the author may adopt a more casual stance towards the audience. If the piece of writing is a story in a book, a business letter or report, or a published article in a journal or if the task is to gain money or support or to get published, the author may adopt a more formal stance. Ultimately, the writer will want to be very careful in how he or she addresses the reader.

Finally, the effectiveness of a piece can be evaluated by asking how well the purpose was achieved. For example, if students are assigned to read a persuasive essay, instructors can ask whether the author influences students' opinions. Students may be assigned two differing persuasive texts with opposing perspectives and be asked which writer was more convincing. Students can then evaluate what factors contributed to this—for example, whether one author uses more credible supporting facts, appeals more effectively to readers' emotions, presents more believable personal anecdotes, or offers stronger

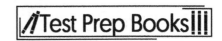

counterargument refutation. Students can then use these evaluations to strengthen their own writing skills.

Using Clear and Coherent Writing

Identifying Details that Develop a Main Idea

The main idea of a piece is the central topic or theme. To identify the main idea, a reader should consider these questions: "What's the point? What does the author want readers to take away from this text?" Everything within the selection should relate back to the main idea because it is the center of the organizational web of any written work. Particularly in articles and reports, the main idea often appears within the opening paragraphs to orient the reader to what the author wants to say about the subject. A sentence that expresses the main idea is known as a thesis sentence or *thesis statement*.

After the main idea has been introduced, *supporting details* are what develop the main idea—they make up the bulk of the work. Without supporting details, the main idea would simply be a statement, so additional details are needed to give that statement weight and validity. Supporting details can often be identified by recognizing the key words that introduce them. The following example offers several supporting details, with key words underlined:

> Man did not evolve from apes. Though we share a common ancestor, humans and apes originated through very different evolutionary paths. There are several reasons why this is true. The <u>first</u> reason is that, logically, if humans evolved from apes, modern-day apes and humans would not coexist. Evolution occurs when a genetic mutation in a species ensures the survival over the rest of the species, allowing them to pass on their genes and create a new lineage of organisms. <u>Another</u> reason is that hominid fossils only fall into one of two categories—ape-like or human-like—and there are very strong differences between the two. Australopithecines, the hominid fossils originally believed to be ancestral to humans, are ape-like, indicated by their long arms, long and curved fingers, and funnel-shaped chests. Their hand bones suggest that they "knuckle-walked" like modern day chimpanzees and gorillas, something not found in *Homo sapien* fossils. <u>Finally</u>, there is no fossilized evidence to suggest a transition between the ape-like ancestor and the *Homo sapien*, indicating that a sudden mutation may have been responsible. These and many other reasons are indicative that humans and ape-like creatures are evolutionarily different.

The underlined words—*first, another,* and *finally*—are the key words that identify the supporting details. These details can be summarized as follows:

- Humans and apes could not coexist.
- Human-like and ape-like fossils are very different.
- No transition is seen between humans and ape-like ancestors.

The supporting details all relate to the central idea that "Man did not evolve from apes," which is the first sentence of the paragraph.

Even though supporting details are more specific than the main idea, they should nevertheless all be directly related to the main idea. Without sufficient supporting details, the writer's main idea will be too weak to be effective.

Organizing a Text Clearly and Coherently

There are five basic elements inherent in effective writing, and each will be discussed throughout the various subheadings of this section.

- *Main idea*: The driving message of the writing, clearly stated or implied

- *Clear organization*: The effective and purposeful arrangement of the content to support the main idea

- *Supporting details/evidence*: Content that gives appropriate depth and weight to the main idea of the story, argument, or information

- *Diction/tone*: The type of language, vocabulary, and word choice used to express the main idea, purposefully aligned to the audience and purpose

- *Adherence to conventions of English*: Correct spelling, grammar, punctuation, and sentence structure, allowing for clear communication of ideas

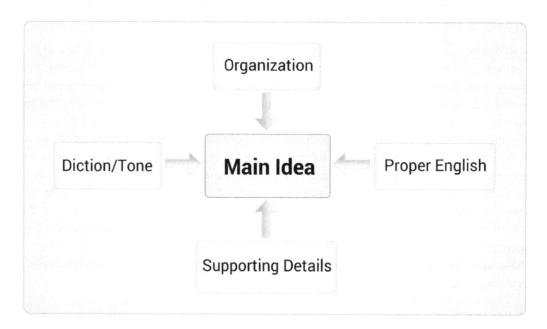

Using Varied and Effective Transitions

Transitions are the glue that holds the writing together. They function to purposefully incorporate new topics and supporting details in a smooth and coherent way. Usually, transitions are found at the beginnings of sentences, but they can also be located in the middle as a way to link clauses together. There are two types of clauses: independent and dependent as discussed in the language use and vocabulary section.

Transition words connect clauses within and between sentences for smoother writing. "I dislike apples. They taste like garbage." is choppier than "I dislike apples because they taste like garbage." Transitions demonstrate the relationship between ideas, allow for more complex sentence structures, and can alert the reader to which type of organizational format the author is using. For example, the above selection on human evolution uses the words *first, another*, and *finally* to indicate that the writer will be listing the reasons why humans and apes are evolutionarily different.

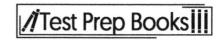

Transition words can be categorized based on the relationships they create between ideas:

- *General order*: signaling elaboration of an idea to emphasize a point—e.g., *for example, for instance, to demonstrate, including, such as, in other words, that is, in fact, also, furthermore, likewise, and, truly, so, surely, certainly, obviously, doubtless*

- *Chronological order*: referencing the time frame in which main event or idea occurs—e.g., *before, after, first, while, soon, shortly thereafter, meanwhile*

- *Numerical order/order of importance*: indicating that related ideas, supporting details, or events will be described in a sequence, possibly in order of importance—e.g., *first, second, also, finally, another, in addition, equally important, less importantly, most significantly, the main reason, last but not least*

- *Spatial order*: referring to the space and location of something or where things are located in relation to each other—e.g., *inside, outside, above, below, within, close, under, over, far, next to, adjacent to*

- *Cause and effect order*: signaling a causal relationship between events or ideas—e.g., *thus, therefore, since, resulted in, for this reason, as a result, consequently, hence, for, so*

- *Compare and contrast order*: identifying the similarities and differences between two or more objects, ideas, or lines of thought—e.g., *like, as, similarly, equally, just as, unlike, however, but, although, conversely, on the other hand, on the contrary*

- *Summary order*: indicating that a particular idea is coming to a close—e.g., *in conclusion, to sum up, in other words, ultimately, above all*

Sophisticated writing also aims to avoid overuse of transitions and ensure that those used are meaningful. Using a variety of transitions makes the writing appear more lively and informed and helps readers follow the progression of ideas.

Justifying Stylistic Choices

Stylistic choices refer to elements such as a writer's diction, sentence structure, and use of figurative language. A writer's *diction* is his or her word choice and may be elevated, academic, conversational, humorous, or any other style. The choice of diction depends on the purpose of a piece of writing. A textbook or a research paper is likely to use academic diction whereas a blog post will use more conversational expressions.

Sentence structure also affects an author's writing style. Will he or she use short, staccato sentences or longer sentences with complex structure? Effective writing tends to incorporate both styles to increase reader interest or to punctuate ideas.

Figurative language includes the use of simile, metaphor, hyperbole, or allusion, to name but a few examples. Creative or descriptive writing is likely to incorporate more non-literal expressions than academic or informative writing will. Instructors should allow students to experiment with different styles of writing and understand how style affects expression and understanding.

Introducing, Developing, and Concluding a Text Effectively

Almost all coherent written works contain three primary parts: a beginning, middle, and end. The organizational arrangements differ widely across distinct writing modes. Persuasive and expository texts utilize an introduction, body, and conclusion whereas narrative works use an orientation, series of events/conflict, and a resolution.

Every element within a written piece relates back to the main idea, and the beginning of a persuasive or expository text generally conveys the main idea or the purpose. For a narrative piece, the beginning is the section that acquaints the reader with the characters and setting, directing them to the purpose of the writing. The main idea in narrative may be implied or addressed at the end of the piece.

Depending on the primary purpose, the arrangement of the middle will adhere to one of the basic organizational structures described in the information texts and rhetoric section. They are cause and effect, problem and solution, compare and contrast, description/spatial, sequence, and order of importance.

The ending of a text is the metaphorical wrap-up of the writing. A solid ending is crucial for effective writing as it ties together loose ends, resolves the action, highlights the main points, or repeats the central idea. A conclusion ensures that readers come away from a text understanding the author's main idea. The table below highlights the important characteristics of each part of a piece of writing.

Structure	Argumentative/Informative	Narrative
Beginning	Introduction *Purpose, main idea*	Orientation *Introduces characters, setting, necessary background*
Middle	Body *Supporting details, reasons and evidence*	Events/Conflict *Story's events that revolve around a central conflict*
End	Conclusion *Highlights main points, summarizes and paraphrases ideas, reiterates the main idea*	Resolution *The solving of the central conflict*

Understanding Effective and Ethical Research Practices

Identifying Relevant Information During Research

Relevant information is that which is pertinent to the topic at hand. Particularly when doing research online, it is easy for students to get overwhelmed with the wealth of information available to them. Before conducting research, then, students need to begin with a clear idea of the question they want to answer.

For example, a student may be interested in learning more about marriage practices in Jane Austen's England. If that student types "marriage" into a search engine, he or she will have to sift through thousands of unrelated sites before finding anything related to that topic. Narrowing down search parameters can aid in locating relevant information.

When using a book, students can consult the table of contents, glossary, or index to discover whether the book contains relevant information before using it as a resource. If the student finds a hefty volume

96

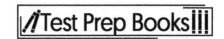

on Jane Austen, he or she can flip to the index in the back, look for the word marriage, and find out how many page references are listed in the book. If there are few or no references to the subject, it is probably not a relevant or useful source.

In evaluating research articles, students may also consult the title, abstract, and keywords before reading the article in its entirety. Referring to the date of publication will also determine whether the research contains up-to-date discoveries, theories, and ideas about the subject, or whether it is outdated.

Evaluating the Credibility of a Print or Digital Source

There are several additional criteria that need to be examined before using a source for a research topic.

The following questions will help determine whether a source is credible:

- Author
  - Who is he or she?
  - Does he or she have the appropriate credentials—e.g., M.D, PhD?
  - Is this person authorized to write on the matter through his/her job or personal experiences?
  - Is he or she affiliated with any known credible individuals or organizations?
  - Has he or she written anything else?
- Publisher
  - Who published/produced the work? Is it a well-known journal, like National Geographic, or a tabloid, like The National Enquirer?
  - Is the publisher from a scholarly, commercial, or government association?
  - Do they publish works related to specific fields?
  - Have they published other works?
  - If a digital source, what kind of website hosts the text? Does it end in .edu, .org, or .com?
- Bias
  - Is the writing objective? Does it contain any loaded or emotional language?
  - Does the publisher/producer have a known bias, such as Fox News or CNN?
  - Does the work include diverse opinions or perspectives?
  - Does the author have any known bias—e.g., Michael Moore, Bill O'Reilly, or the Pope? Is he or she affiliated with any organizations or individuals that may have a known bias—e.g., Citizens United or the National Rifle Association?
  - Does the magazine, book, journal, or website contain any advertising?
- References
  - Are there any references?
  - Are the references credible? Do they follow the same criteria as stated above?
  - Are the references from a related field?
- Accuracy/reliability
  - Has the article, book, or digital source been peer reviewed?
  - Are all of the conclusions, supporting details, or ideas backed with published evidence?
  - If a digital source, is it free of grammatical errors, poor spelling, and improper English?
  - Do other published individuals have similar findings?
- Coverage
  - Are the topic and related material both successfully addressed?
  - Does the work add new information or theories to those of their sources?
  - Is the target audience appropriate for the intended purpose?

Identifying Effective Research Practices

The purpose of all research is to provide an answer to an unknown question. Therefore, all good research papers pose the topic in the form of a question, which they will then seek to answer with clear ideas, arguments, and supporting evidence.

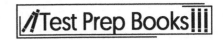

A *research question* is the primary focus of the research piece, and it should be formulated on a unique topic. To formulate a research question, writers begin by choosing a general topic of interest and then research the literature to determine what sort of research has already been done—the *literature review*. This helps them narrow the topic into something original and determine what still needs to be asked and researched about the topic. A solid question is very specific and avoids generalizations. The following question is offered for evaluation:

> *What is most people's favorite kind of animal?*

This research question is extremely broad without giving the paper any particular focus—it could go any direction and is not an exceptionally unique focus. To narrow it down, the question could consider a specific population:

> *What is the favorite animal of people in Ecuador?*

While this question is better, it does not address exactly why this research is being conducted or why anyone would care about the answer. Here's another possibility:

> *What does the animal considered as the most favorite of people in different regions throughout Ecuador reveal about their socioeconomic status?*

This question is extremely specific and gives a very clear direction of where the paper or project is going to go. However, sometimes the question can be too limited, where very little research has been conducted to create a solid paper, and the researcher most likely does not have the means to travel to Ecuador and travel door-to-door conducting a census on people's favorite animals. In this case, the research question would need to be broadened. Broadening a topic can mean introducing a wider range of criteria. Instead of people in Ecuador, the topic could be opened to include the population of South America or expanded to include more issues or considerations.

Identifying the Components of a Citation
Citation styles vary according to which style guide is consulted. Examples of commonly-used styles include MLA, APA, and Chicago/Turabian. Each citation style includes similar components, although the order and formatting of these components varies.

MLA Style
For an MLA style citation, components must be included or excluded depending on the source, so writers should determine which components are applicable to the source being cited. Here are the basic components:

- Author—last name, first name
- Title of source
- Title of container—e.g., a journal title or website
- Other contributors—e.g., editor or translator
- Version
- Number
- Publisher
- Publication date
- Location—e.g., the URL or DOI
- Date of Access—optional

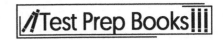

99

APA Style

The following components can be found in APA style citations. Components must be included or excluded depending on the source, so writers should determine which components are applicable to the source being cited.

The basic components are as follows:

- Author—last name, first initial, middle initial
- Publication date
- Title of chapter, article, or text
- Editor— last name, first initial, middle initial
- Version/volume
- Number/issue
- Page numbers
- DOI or URL
- Database—if article is difficult to locate
- City of publication
- State of publication, abbreviated
- Publisher

Chicago/Turabian Style

Chicago/Turabian style citations are also referred to as note systems and are used most frequently in the humanities and the arts. Components must be included or excluded depending on the source, so writers should determine which components are applicable to the source being cited. They contain the following elements:

- Author—last name, first name, middle initial
- Title of chapter or article—in quotation marks
- Title of source
- Editor—first name, last name
- Page numbers
- Version/volume
- Number/issue
- Page numbers
- Date of access
- DOI
- Publication location—city and state abbreviation/country
- Publisher
- Publication Date

Citing Source Material Appropriately

The following information contains examples of the common types of sources used in research as well as the formats for each citation style. First lines of citation entries are presented flush to the left margin,

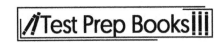

and second/subsequent details are presented with a hanging indent. Some examples of bibliography entries are presented below:

Book
- MLA
  Format: Last name, First name, Middle initial. *Title of Source*. Publisher, Publication Date.
  Example: Sampson, Maximus R. *Diaries from an Alien Invasion*. Campbell Press, 1989.
- APA
  Format: Last name, First initial, Middle initial. (Year Published) *Book Title*. City, State: Publisher.
  Example: Sampson, M. R. (1989). *Diaries from an Alien Invasion. Springfield, IL*: Campbell Press.
- Chicago/Turabian
  Format: Last name, First name, Middle initial. *Book Title*. City, State: Publisher, Year of publication.
  Example: Sampson, Maximus R. *Diaries from an Alien Invasion. Springfield, IL*: Campbell Press, 1989.

A Chapter in an Edited Book
- MLA
  Format: Last name, First name, Middle initial. "Title of Source." *Title of Container*, Other Contributors, Publisher, Publication Date, Location.
  Example: Sampson, Maximus R. "The Spaceship." *Diaries from an Alien Invasion*, edited by Allegra M. Brewer, Campbell Press, 1989, pp. 45-62.
- APA
  Format: Last name, First Initial, Middle initial. (Year Published) Chapter title. In First initial, Middle initial, Last Name (Ed.), *Book title* (pp. page numbers). City, State: Publisher.
  Example: Sampson, M. R. (1989). The Spaceship. In A. M. Brewer (Ed.), *Diaries from an Alien Invasion* (pp. 45-62). Springfield, IL: Campbell Press.
- Chicago/Turabian
  Format: Last name, First name, Middle initial. "Chapter Title." In Book Title, edited by Editor's Name (First, Middle In. Last), Page(s). City: Publisher, Year Published.
  Example: Sampson, Maximus R. "The Spaceship," in *Diaries from an Alien Invasion*, edited by Allegra M. Brewer, 45-62. Springfield: Campbell Press, 1989.

Article in a Journal
- MLA
  Format: Last name, First name, Middle initial. "Title of Source." *Title of Container*, Number, Publication Date, Location.
  Example: Rowe, Jason R. "The Grief Monster." *Strong Living*, vol. 9, no. 9, 2016, pp 25-31.
- APA
  Format: Last name, First initial, Middle initial. (Year Published). Title of article. *Name of Journal, volume*(issue), page(s).
  Example: Rowe, J. R. (2016). The grief monster. *Strong Living, 9*(9), 25-31.
- Chicago/Turabian:
  Format: Last name, First name, Middle initial. "Title of Article." *Name of Journal* volume, issue (Year Published): Page(s).
  Example: Rowe, Jason, R. "The Grief Monster." *Strong Living* 9, no. 9 (2016): 25-31.

Page on a Website
- MLA
  Format: Last name, First name, Middle initial. "Title of Article." *Name of Website*, date published (Day Month Year), URL. Date accessed (Day Month Year).
  Example: Rowe, Jason. "The Grief Monster." *Strong Living Online*, 9 Sept. 2016. http://www.somanylosses.com/the-grief-monster/html. Accessed 13 Sept. 2016.
- APA
  Format: Last name, First initial. Middle initial. (Date Published—Year, Month Day). Page or article title. Retrieved from URL
  Example: Rowe, J. W. (2016, Sept. 9). The grief monster. Retrieved from http://www.somanylosses.com/ the-grief-monster/html
- Chicago/Turabian
  Format: Last Name, First Name, Middle initial. "Page Title." *Website Title*. Last modified Month day, year. Accessed month, day, year. URL.
  Example: Rowe, Jason. "The Grief Monster." *Strong Living Online*. Last modified September 9, 2016. Accessed September 13, 2016. http://www.somany losses.com/the-grief-monster/html.

In-Text Citations

Most of the content found in a research paper will be supporting evidence that must be cited in-text, i.e., directly after the sentence that makes the statement. In-text citations contain details that correspond to the first detail in the bibliography entry—usually the author.

- MLA style - In-text citations will contain the author and the page number (if the source has page numbers) for direct quotations. Paraphrased source material may have just the author.
  - According to Johnson, liver cancer treatment is "just beyond our reach" (976).
  - The treatment of liver cancer is not within our reach, currently (Johnson).
  - The narrator opens the story with a paradoxical description: "It was the best of times, it was the worst of times" (Dickens 1).
- APA Style - In text citations will contain the author, the year of publication, and a page marker—if the source is paginated—for direct quotations. Paraphrased source material will include the author and year of publication.
  - According to Johnson (1986), liver cancer treatment is "just beyond our reach" (p. 976).
  - The treatment of liver cancer is not within our reach, currently (Johnson, 1986).
- Chicago Style - Chicago style has two approaches to in-text citation: notes and bibliography or author-date.
  - Notes – There are two options for notes: endnotes—provided in a sequential list at the end of the paper and separate from bibliography—or footnotes provided at the bottom of a page. In either case, the use of superscript indicates the citation number.
    - Johnson states that treatment of liver cancer is "just beyond our reach."[1]
    - 1. Robert W. Johnson, Oncology in the Twenty-first Century (Kentville, Nova Scotia: Kentville Publishing, 1986), 159.
  - Author-Date – The author-date system includes the author's name, publication year, and page number.
    - Johnson states that treatment of liver cancer is "just beyond our reach" (1986, 159).
    - Research shows that liver cancer treatment is not within our reach, currently (Johnson 1986, 159).

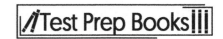

Integrating Information from Source Material

It can be daunting to integrate so many sources into a research paper while still maintaining fluency and coherency. Most source material is incorporated in the form of quotations or paraphrases, while citing the source at the end of their respective references. There are several guidelines to consider when integrating a source into writing:

- The piece should be written in the author's voice. Quotations, especially long ones, should be limited and spaced evenly throughout the paper.

- All paragraphs should begin with the author's own words and end with his or her own words; quotations should never start or end a paragraph.

- Quotations and paraphrases should be used to emphasize a point, give weight to an idea, and validate a claim.

- Supporting evidence should be introduced in a sentence or paragraph, and then explained afterwards: *According to Waters (1979)* [signal phrase], *"All in all, we're just another brick in the wall" (p.24). The wall suggests that people are becoming more alienated, and the bricks symbolize a paradoxical connection to that alienation* [Explanation].

- When introducing a source for the first time, the author's name and a smooth transition should be included: *In Pink Floyd's groundbreaking album The Wall, Roger Waters argues that society is causing people to become more alienated.*

- There should be an even balance between quotations and paraphrases.

- Quotations or paraphrases should never be taken out of context in a way that alters the original author's intent.

- Quotations should be syntactically and grammatically integrated.

- Quotations should not simply be copied and pasted in the paper, rather, they should be introduced into a paper with natural transitions.

  - As argued in Johnson's article…
  - Evidence of this point can be found in Johnson's article, where she asserts that…
  - The central argument of John's article is…

Using Effective Speech and Presentation Delivery

Understanding Effective Delivery of a Speech or Presentation

Good public speakers all have several characteristics in common. It is not enough to simply write a speech, but it must also be delivered in a manner that is both engaging and succinct. The following qualities are inherent to good public speaking.

Confidence is possibly the most important attribute a speaker can have. It instills trust in the listener that the person knows what he or she is talking about and that he or she is credible and competent. Confidence is displayed by making brief eye contact—about 2-3 seconds—with different members of the audience to demonstrate that the speaker is engaged. It is also displayed in his or her tone of voice—strong, light-hearted, and natural. A nervous speaker can easily be identified by a small, quivering voice. Confidence is also conveyed by the speaker facing the audience; turning one's back may demonstrate insecurity.

Authenticity is another quality of an effective speaker, as it makes a person more relatable and believable to the audience. Speeches that are memorized word-for-word can give the impression of being inauthentic as the monologue does not flow quite naturally, especially if the speaker accidentally fumbles or forgets. Memorizing speeches can also lead to a monotonous tone, which is sure to put the audience to sleep, or worse, a misinterpreted tone, which can cause the audience to stop listening entirely or even become offended. Therefore, speeches should be practiced with a natural intonation and not be memorized mechanically.

Connection with the audience is another important aspect of public speaking. Speakers should engage with their listeners by the use of storytelling and visual or auditory aids, as well as asking questions that the audience can participate in. Visual and auditory aids could range from an interesting PowerPoint presentation to a short video clip to physical objects the audience can pass around to a soundtrack. The use of appropriate humor also allows the audience to connect with the speaker on a more personal level and will make the speech sound more like a conversation than a one-sided lecture. Speakers who are passionate about their subject inspire their listeners to care about what they're saying; they transfer their energy into the audience. This level of connection will encourage their listeners to want to be there.

Succinctness and *purposeful repetition* ensures that the audience's attention remains focused on the message at hand. Repeating the overall point of the speech in different ways helps listeners remember what the speaker is trying to tell them, even when the speech is over. A speech that is longer than necessary will cause listeners to become bored and stop absorbing information. Keeping the speech short and sweet and leaving more time for questions at the end will ensure that the audience stays engaged.

There are many different styles a speaker can utilize, but the most important thing speakers should keep in mind is maintaining a connection with the audience. This will help ensure that the audience will remain open and focused enough to hear and absorb the message.

Evaluating the Advantages and Disadvantages of Different Media

Each visual aid has its advantages and disadvantages and should be used sparingly to avoid distracting the audience. Visual aids should be used to emphasize a presentation's message, not overwhelm it.

Microsoft PowerPoint is currently the most commonly used visual aid. It allows for pictures, words, videos, and music to be presented on the same screen and is essentially just a projection of a computer screen, allowing easy and quick access to all forms of media as well as the Internet. However, a PowerPoint presentation should not be overwhelmed with information, such as text-heavy slides, as audience members will spend more time reading the slides than listening to the speaker. Conversely, they may avoid reading it entirely, and the presentation will serve no purpose. A PowerPoint presentation that uses too many animations and visual elements may also detract from the presence of the speaker.

Handouts are a great way for the audience to feel more involved in a presentation. They can present lots of information that may be too much for a PowerPoint, and they can also be taken home and reviewed later. The primary disadvantage of handouts is that the audience may choose to read rather than to listen, thus missing the main points the speaker is trying to make, or they may decide not to read it at

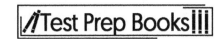

all. The best handouts are those that do not contain all the information of a presentation, but allow for the audience to take notes and complete the handout by listening or asking questions.

Whiteboards and *blackboards* are excellent for explaining difficult concepts by allowing the audience to follow along with a process and copy down their own version of what is being written on the board. This visual aid is best used to explain concepts in mathematics and science. The main problem with the board, however, is that there can be limited space, and if the presenter runs out of room, he or she will have to erase the content written on the board and will be unable to refer back to it later. He or she may also have to wait for the entire audience to write the information down, which slows down the presentation.

Overhead projectors are wonderful in that a speaker can use a prepared transparency and draw images or add words to emphasize or explain concepts. They can also erase these additions but still keep the original content if they wish to alter their method to fit the audience or provide further explanations. Similar to PowerPoint presentations, overhead projections should limit the amount of text to keep the audience focused on listening.

Physical objects are a useful way to connect with the audience and allow them to feel more involved. Because people interact with the physical world, physical objects can help solidify understanding of difficult concepts. However, they can be distracting if not properly introduced. If they are presented too early or are visible during the presentation, the audience will focus on the objects, wondering what purpose they may serve instead of listening to the speaker. Objects should instead be hidden until it is time to show them and then collected when they are no longer useful.

Videos are a great way to enliven a presentation by giving it sound, music, flow, and images. They are excellent for emphasizing points, providing evidence for ideas, giving context, or setting tone. The major issue with videos is that the presenter is unable to speak at this point, so this form of media should be used sparingly and purposefully. Also, overly-long videos may lose the audience's attention.

Effective public speakers are aware of the advantages and disadvantages of all forms of media and often choose to utilize a combination of several different types to keep the presentations lively and the audience engaged.

Presenting Information Clearly, Concisely, and Logically

All information should be presented with a clear beginning, middle, and end. Distinct organization always makes any work more clear, concise, and logical. For a presentation, this should involve choosing a primary topic and then discussing it in the following format:

- Introducing the speaker and the main topic
- Providing evidence, supporting details, further explanation of the topic in the main body
- Concluding it with a firm resolution and repetition of the main point

The beginning, middle, and end should also be linked with effective transitions that make the presentation flow well. For example, a presentation should always begin with an introduction by the speaker, including what he/she does and what he/she is there to present. Good transitional introductions may begin with statements such as *For those who do not know me, my name is...*, *As many of you know, I am...* or *Good morning everyone, my name is ___, and I am the new project manager.* A good introduction grabs the attention and interest of the audience.

After an introduction has been made, the speaker will then want to state the purpose of the presentation with a natural transition, such as *I am here to discuss the latest editions to our standard of procedure...* or *This afternoon, I would like to present the results of our latest findings*. Once the purpose has been identified, the speaker will want to adhere to the main idea announced. The presenter should be certain to keep the main idea to one sentence as too much information can confuse an audience; an introduction should be succinct and to the point.

Supporting information should always be presented in concise, easy-to-read formats such as bullet points or lists—if visual aids are presented during the presentation. Good transitions such as *Let's begin with...* or *Now to look at...* make the presentation flow smoothly and logically, helping listeners to keep ideas organized as they are presented. Keeping the material concise is extremely important in a presentation, and visual aids should be used only to emphasize points or explain ideas. All the supporting information should relate back to the main idea, avoiding unnecessary tangents.

Finally, a firm conclusion involves repeating the main point of the presentation by either inspiring listeners to act or by reiterating the most important points made in the speech. It should also include an expression of gratitude to the audience as well as transition to opening the floor for questions.

Instructing Students on the Effective Use of Digital Media

Using Technology Tools for Effective Communication
Different technological tools serve different functions. To function in the developing world, students need to learn and understand *digital literacy*—the knowledge, dexterity, and critical thinking skills involved in using technology to create, evaluate, and present information. The best techniques for instructing students on choosing and using technological tools involve educating them on the advantages and disadvantages of each, demonstrating how to use them, breaking down their different aspects, assigning students homework or projects in which they will utilize different technological resources, and instructing them on when it is appropriate to use each kind. The most common types of tools used for communication are as follows:

- Smartphones/apps
- Email
- Microsoft Office
- iMovie
- Skype
- Twitter
- Facebook
- Instagram
- Google Drive
- Various blogging websites
- Online bulletin boards
- Wikis

A good way to introduce students to varying technological tools is by using them in the classroom. It would be helpful to teach students how to use a PowerPoint presentation, for example, by giving a PowerPoint presentation. If a student asks a question to which the teacher does not know the answer, they can discover the answer together by using a reliable source on the Internet, projecting the process on the board, so that they can see exactly how it's done. Students can also receive homework and

updates on school and classroom events through a personal blog or class bulletin board the teacher has designed so that they may become familiar with using online communication. Students can also be assigned to use personal blogs to practice and improve their writing skills.

The most effective method for learning new skills is a hands-on approach. Students can be educated on the pros and cons of each technological tool, but the best way for them to learn is to allow them to find out for themselves by assigning projects and asking them to give the reasoning behind choosing a specific tool. For example, they may be asked to do a project on some aspect of the Revolutionary War by choosing a media format. Ideas may include the following:

- Doing a presentation
- Filming and editing a video re-enactment of a great battle
- Writing a script in Microsoft Word or in a Google doc and having classmates act it out
- Creating Facebook statuses from the viewpoints of the forefathers in modern colloquial language
- Having a "Twitter war" between the British and the Colonials
- Asking various people to participate in a collaborative Wiki or Google Doc in which many people give their versions of aspects of the Revolutionary War
- Writing a blog narrating life as a soldier
- Posting photos of the signing of the Declaration of Independence

Students can then give their presentations to the classroom so that students can learn about the topic through different presentation styles.

Another way to engage students in using technology is to have them communicate with each other through the various methods of communication—e.g., starting a class Google Doc, creating a classroom Facebook group, or using a discussion board. This is also an excellent opportunity to encourage students to use Standard English through all methods of communication to enhance their writing skills and instill a sense of professionalism, which they will need throughout their lives.

For example, requiring that all students use complete sentences, proper spelling, and grammar through Facebook, Twitter, or blogs associated with homework or projects will encourage them to do so in their daily lives as well. Another example is requiring that students select tweets from their favorite celebrities or politicians, analyze their meaning and purpose, correct their grammar and spelling, and re-tweet them in the correct way. There are countless ways in which technology can be used in the classroom to enhance students' understanding of digital communication; all it requires is a little creativity.

Evaluating Technology-Based Strategies

It is hard to find a technological tool that will not be useful for students to explore. The more a student engages with the numerous different types of technology, the more digitally literate that student will become. Each type is effective and brings value to the table in its own way. When evaluating the effectiveness of a specific technology-based strategy, it's important to consider how this method is enhancing the student's digital literacy, as well as their critical thinking and communication skills.

It is also necessary to evaluate the technology itself by asking relevant questions:

- Is it appropriate for the average age of the students in the classroom?
- Is it user friendly?
- Does it work consistently?
- Are there multiple ways to get help on learning how to use it?
- Are there trouble-shooting options?
- Does it have good reviews?
- Is it relevant to the content of the curriculum?
- Does it support and align to the learning objective?
- Is it more distracting than it is useful?
- Is it a tool that is/will be used often in the real world?
- Can it be used for more than one project or assignment?

One very effective teaching strategy is *collaborative learning*, in which two or more students work together to develop a project, work through an idea, or solve a problem. This method allows for students to play off each other's strengths and different experiences and learn how to communicate with their classmates to achieve goals. Technology can be used for collaborative learning in Google Drive, Skype, Google Hangouts, Neapod, Padlet, and Periscope, in creating PowerPoint presentations together, or by conducting surveys with websites like Survey Monkey.

Another effective teaching method is *discussion*, in which students are given a topic or create a topic themselves and then use technology to engage in discourse. This can be done via discussion boards, such as ProBoards or Boardhost, or done live through programs such as Skype or Hangouts. Discussion strategies are extremely effective for enhancing communication skills and digital literacy.

A third method is *active learning*, in which the student engages in activities such as reading, writing, or teaching the subject to another student. Blogging is a great way to encourage active learning as it provides a medium through which students can reflect on what they've learned and respond to comments posted by the teacher or other students. Most of the suggestions made in the previous section—making presentations, creating video re-enactments, writing scripts, having mock Twitter or Facebook comment wars—are all forms of active learning. These types of activities solidify events, ideas, and skills in a student's mind in a way that memorization or flashcards do not as they utilize many different types of thinking and interaction.

One method that a teacher may employ depending on the class and circumstances is *distance learning*. Distance learning is any type of teaching method in which the student and teacher are not in the same place simultaneously. Many professors utilize distance learning through different kinds of technologies, including a live virtual lecture, computer simulations, interactive discussions, and virtual/audio learning environments. These strategies have their advantages in that one teacher can teach a large number of students and multiple locations, and students can communicate with fellow classmates across the globe.

Auditory learning is a strategy in which a student learns through listening. This typically happens via recorded lectures that can be downloaded as podcasts onto a classroom website, discussion board, or some other audio-simulated learning environment. *Visual learning* is learning through watching, in which ideas and concepts are illustrated through images, videos, or by observing a teacher complete a task, explain a concept, or solve a problem. This can be achieved through recorded videos, cartoons, virtual lectures, or by sitting in the classroom. Additionally, *kinesthetic learning* is active learning through

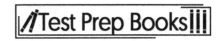

physical interaction with an object or actively solving a problem, as opposed to passively listening or watching.

Every student has a different learning style which is unique to them—some learn better through listening while others learn better through doing. The best teaching methods employ all different learning strategies so that all the senses are engaged and every student has a chance at learning material based on their individual learning needs. Technology offers educators the tools do that.

Understanding Research-Based Approaches to Teaching Components of Writing

Recognizing Research-Based Strategies for Teaching the Writing Process

Current trends in education have recognized the need to cultivate writing skills that prepare students for higher education and professional careers. To this end, writing skills are being integrated into other subjects beyond the language arts classroom. The skills and strategies used in language arts class, then, should be adaptable for other learning tasks. In this way, students can achieve greater proficiency by incorporating writing strategies into every aspect of learning.

To teach writing, it is important that writers know the writing process. Students should be familiar with the five components of the writing process:

1. *Pre-writing*: The drafting, planning, researching, and brainstorming of ideas
2. *Writing*: The part of the project in which the actual, physical writing takes place
3. *Revising*: Adding to, removing, rearranging, or re-writing sections of the piece
4. *Editing*: Analyzing and correcting mistakes in grammar, spelling, punctuation, formatting, and word choice
5. *Publishing*: Distributing the finished product to the teacher, employer, or other students

The *writing workshop* is possibly the most common approach to teaching writing. It is an organized approach in which the student is guided by the teacher and usually contains the following components:

- *Short lesson* (~10 min) in which the teacher focuses on a particular aspect of the writing process—e.g., strategies, organization, technique, processes, craft—and gives explicit instructions for the task at hand

- *Independent writing time* (~30 min) in which the student engages in the writing activity and works through the process while receiving help from the teacher, writing in his/her own style on either a chosen topic or one assigned, and engaging with other students

- *Sharing* (~10 min) in which the student shares a piece of his or her work, either in a small group or as a class, and gains insight by listening to the work of other students

Another common strategy is *teacher modeling*, in which the student views the teacher as a writer and is therefore more apt to believe the teacher's instruction on the subject. To be a good writing teacher, the teacher must be a good writer. Therefore, it is important that the teacher practice his or her own writing on a somewhat regular basis through blogging, journaling, or creative writing, in order to keep his or her skills sharp.

The following are some strategies for teacher writing:

- *Sharing written work*: This strategy is a good audio and/or visual learning technique. The teacher should frequently share personal writing with students so that the student recognizes the instructor as having authority on the subject. Many teachers also encourage feedback from the students to stimulate critical thinking skills.

- *Writing in front of students*: This strategy is very effective as a visual learning technique as the students watch as the teacher works through the writing process. This could include asking the students to provide a question or topic on which to write and then writing on blackboard or projector.

- *Encouraging real-world writing*: This is a kinesthetic teaching strategy in which the teacher urges students to write as frequently as possible and to share their written work with other students or an authentic audience. Teachers may also find it beneficial to show students their own blogs and other online media to demonstrate exactly how it's done. Students may also choose to model their writing after a published author, imitating his or her style, sentence structure, and word choices to become comfortable with the writing process.

Finally, a good thing for a student to have is a *writer's notebook*, which contains all the student's written work over the course of the curriculum, including warm-up assignments, drafts, brainstorming templates, and completed works. This allows the student to review previous writing assignment, learn from their mistakes, and see concrete evidence for improvement. Depending on the age group, many of the assignments could be performed on a word processor to encourage computer literacy.

Identifying Strategies for Teaching Writing Tasks

There are over thirty research-proven strategies for teaching all components of the writing process through a variety of different tasks, the most comprehensive of which will be covered in this section.

Evidence shows that the most effective strategy for teaching writing is to have the students use the process-writing approach, in which they practice planning, writing, reviewing, editing, and publishing their work. Students should be taught how to write for a specific audience, take personal responsibility for their own work, and participate in the writing process with other students, such as a discussion-like setting where they can brainstorm together.

Additionally, specific goals should be assigned, either classroom wide or to fit individual needs, through activities that encourage attention to spelling, grammar, sentence combination, and writing for specific audiences.

- For pre-writing, students should also be exposed to the process of generating and organizing ideas before they set pen to paper, such as being given a specific topic and considering many different aspects associated with that topic using a *brainstorming web* or *mindmap*, visually dividing a project into main topics and subtopics. Teachers can help students by encouraging them to explore what they already know about a subject, topic, or genre. They can then illustrate how to go about researching and gathering information or data by using teacher modeling to access a variety of resources. Another research-based strategy is to require students to analyze and summarize a model text through writing, which encourages them to condense a composition into its main ideas and, in doing so, allows them to understand how these ideas were expressed and organized.

- To teach the actual act of writing, *freewriting* is an effective writing warm-up activity as it requires nothing more than for the student to continually write uninterrupted for an allotted amount of time. One of the most common problems many students encounter is being uncertain what to write or how to begin. Freewriting creates a space in which the student does not have to worry about either of those things—they simply need to write. For this particular strategy, a teacher should avoid assigning a particular topic, genre, or format, nor should the student be encouraged or required to share what they have written so that they may write freely and without fear of judgment. After the allotted time for freewriting is up, students can then read back over what they have written and select the most interesting sentences and ideas to expand upon in a more organized piece of writing.

Another form of instruction is *discipline-based inquiry*, which encourages students to analyze writing models in a particular mode to better grasp the characteristics of that style. For example, before assigning students a persuasive writing assignment, an instructor would first give several samples of persuasive passages to students and ask them to read the texts carefully, paying attention to components such as diction—what kind of emotional or connotative language the writer uses to subtly influence readers' opinion, supporting arguments—how the writer integrates objective data to support a subjective argument, and organization—how the writer presents the information and argument. By focusing students' attention on a specific writing mode, the instructor allows students to use their analytical and observation skills to formulate an idea about the prominent characteristics of a particular mode of writing.

In *Self-Regulated Strategy Development* (SRSD), instructors progressively instill independent skills in students by first prompting students for their prior knowledge about a subject, building on that background knowledge, instructing them more deeply in strategies related to the learning objective, and then practicing the strategy enough times so that it becomes an embedded habit in students' learning process.

Finally, encouraging students to write with one another in a collaborative setting is a good way to enhance revision, editing, and publishing skills by learning, discussing, and writing for each other. By giving constructive feedback to their peers, students learn how to recognize and apply standards of effective writing, and they also become more skilled at troubleshooting and making corrections when problems occur in the writing process.

Interpreting and Applying Research to Writing Challenges

Teaching writing to many students can be challenging as they all possess individual needs, individual learning styles, and individual emotional responses to feedback. There is no one way to teach writing that will address the needs of every student, and the techniques may vary between genres, topics, and audiences. However, teachers should keep in mind the five fundamental criteria, which research has shown to be most effective.

The most important way a student learns is by doing—being given as many opportunities to write as possible. Activities such a pre-writing, writing on prompts, peer revision, and writing in groups should be implemented as often as possible in many different types of subjects.

A welcoming, encouraging, and judgment-free atmosphere is the most conducive environment for learning how to write, where students can feel comfortable in engaging in activities, sharing what they have written, brainstorming ideas, providing feedback to peers, and giving/receiving mutual respect.

Feedback should be specific and individualized—teachers must provide sufficient time to students to help them reach their writing goals and improve on their weaknesses, while also being mindful of students' responses to criticism. At the same time, teachers should give students the tools they need to self-evaluate their own writing and identify areas of improvement.

Strategies for teaching writing should be varied and comprehensive. Teachers should be able to adjust their pedagogical techniques to meet individualized needs while still maintaining the fundamental approaches to teaching all elements of the writing process.

Learning is often achieved through writing—not only of the writing process, but of all subjects in general. Keeping a reflective journal of what they have learned at school encourages students to learn the material as they must make sense of it through writing it down. Having a student write on a historical event or a scientific theory provides the same advantage. Writing skills learned in a language arts class can and should be utilized in other subject areas.

While there are many challenges to teaching a range of students, each student can have his or her learning needs met if the teacher utilizes all five of these methods in his or her instructional approaches.

Assessing Reading, Writing, Speaking, and Listening

Identifying Research-Based Approaches to Formative and Summative Assessment

It is almost as important to provide feedback and evaluate a student's skill level as it is to teach. Most classes utilize both formative and summative assessments as a grading template. Although assessment and grading are not the same thing, assessments are often used to award a grade. A *formative assessment* monitors the student's progress in learning and allows continuous feedback throughout the course in the form of homework and in-class assignments, such as quizzes, writing workshops, conferences, or inquiry-based writing prompts. These assessments typically make up a lower percent of the overall grade. Alternatively, a *summative assessment* compares a student's progress in learning against some sort of standard, such as against the progress of other students or by the number of correct answers. These assessments usually make up a higher percent of the overall grade and come in the form of midterm or final exams, papers, or major projects.

One evidence-based method used to assess a student's progress is a rubric. A *rubric* is an evaluation tool that explicitly states the expectations of the assignment and breaks it down into different components.

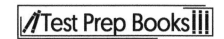

Each component has a clear description and relationship to the assignment as a whole. For writing, rubrics may be *holistic*, judging the overall quality of the writing, or they can be *analytic*, in which different aspects of the writing are evaluated, e.g., structure, style, word choices, and punctuation.

Rubrics can be used in all aspects of a curriculum, including reading comprehension, oral presentations, speeches, performances, papers, projects, and listening comprehension. They are usually formative in nature, but can be summative depending on the purpose. Rubrics allow instructors to provide specific feedback and allow students to understand the expectations for an assignment.

An example of an analytic rubric is displayed below:

Name _____   Date _____

Essay Rubric	4 Mastery	3 Satisfactory	2 Needs Improvement	1 Poor
Writing Quality	-Excellent usage of voice and style -Outstanding organizational skills -Wealth of relevant information	-Style and voice of essay was interesting -Mostly organized -Useful amount of information	-Inconsistent style and voice -Lacked clear organization -Small amount of useful information	-No noticeable style or voice -Virtually no organization -No relevant information
Grammar Conventions	-Essentially no mistakes in grammar -Correct spelling throughout	-Minor amount of grammar and spelling mistakes	-Many errors in grammar conventions and spelling	-Too many grammatical errors to understand the meaning of the piece

Another research-proven strategy is *conferencing*, in which students participate in a group discussion that usually involves the teacher. Students learn best when they can share their thoughts on what they've read or written and receive feedback from their peers and instructors. For writing, conferencing is frequently done in the revision stage. Through discussion, students are also able to enhance their listening and speaking skills. Conferences can be done in a one-on-one setting, typically between a student and instructor, or in a small group of students with guidance from the instructor. They are useful in that they provide an atmosphere of respect where a student can share his or her work and thoughts without fear of judgment. They increase motivation and allow students to explore a variety of topics and discussions. Conferences also allow the instructor to provide immediate feedback or prompt students for deeper explanations of their ideas.

The most successful conferences have these characteristics:

- Have a set structure
- Focus on only a few points—too many are confusing or distracting
- Are solution based
- Allow students to both discuss their thoughts/works and receive/provide feedback for others
- Encourage the use of appropriate vocabulary
- Provide motivation and personal satisfaction or pleasure from reading and writing
- Allow a time where questions can be asked and immediately answered

Rubrics and conferencing are both methods that provide useful *feedback*, one of the most important elements in the progress of a student's learning. Feedback is essentially corrective instruction delivered in writing, either verbally or non-verbally. Research has shown that the following techniques are the most effective when giving feedback:

Being specific

For a student to know exactly how he or she is doing, feedback should be directed towards specific components of a student's writing, listening, or speaking skills, not a holistic overview. For example, writing "Excellent!" on a student's paper or homework is not useful information as it's unclear what was done well. A paper should provide useful comments throughout the body of the work, for example, "Wording is confusing here," or "Great use of adjectives." However, instructor comments should not overwhelm the student's writing; they should be used to focus their attention on specific areas of success or improvement. This encourages the student to keep doing what he or she is doing well and work on what needs improvement without being overwhelmed.

Being sensitive

Giving feedback is precarious in nature as it entirely depends upon the emotional and mental states of the receiver. Some students do well with "tough love," while others may be discouraged and disheartened to see a slew of comments on their paper. Teachers should pay attention to how a student reacts to feedback. As a general rule, feedback should focus more on the positives so as not to damage self-esteem, while teaching students new techniques for self-correction, instead of simply criticizing what they've done. Also, it's important to try and be aware of the types of feedback each student responds the most effectively to, for example, providing oral feedback for students who don't read well.

Being Prompt

Feedback should be presented sooner rather than later, so that students will not have time to repeat mistakes they are unaware of that may become habitual. Studies have shown that students who are given immediate feedback display a greater increase in performance than those who were given feedback later in the term. As soon as the action has happened, it is important give the appropriate praise or critique so that the student associates the feedback with the action.

Being Explicit

It is important to explain the purpose of the feedback before it is given so that a student does not feel controlled, too closely examined, or competitive. This can cause the learner to feel self-conscious and discourage him or her from performing his or her best. The importance of feedback and how it is meant to improve on a personal skill set should be explained to the student.

Being Focused

Teachers should try and keep the feedback in alignment with the goal the student is expected to achieve. Too much feedback, especially if it is unrelated to the goal, can be overwhelming and distracting from the purpose of the assignment or paper.

Here are some other tips to consider when giving feedback:

- Teachers should be aware of their body language and facial expressions when giving feedback—a frown or grimace can be very discouraging, even if the written feedback was mostly positive.

- It's conducive to concentrate on one thing at a time. If a student submits a paper with a lot of errors, for example, it may be helpful to identify a prevalent pattern of error and work through strategies to correct it so that student does not feel overwhelmed.

- Using effective rubrics can make all the difference—letting students know exactly what is expected will provide them with a basis on which to model their techniques and skills.

- Students should be educated on giving feedback. This can be demonstrated by example and through instruction how to give feedback in a positive, constructive way and correct any behavior that trends toward disrespect or excessive competition. Students should also provide feedback to the teacher as well.

- Teachers should not give the same comments to every student, but make them personal.

- When offering criticism, teachers should always offer tips for how the student can improve.

- It's important to avoid personal comments, e.g., "You're so smart!" or "Math isn't your best subject." Rather, the comments should focus on the writing: e.g., "The organization of this paper is clear."

- Students shouldn't be compared to each other, e.g., "Look how perfectly Victor composed this sentence!" This can galvanize the students into competing with one another.

Evaluating the Effectiveness of Research-Based Approaches to Formative and Summative Assessment

Most research has already been done to evaluate the effectiveness of certain strategies of formative and summative assessments. Because there are innumerable approaches to the art of teaching, the only real way one can evaluate a strategy's effectiveness is to monitor how the students improve over time with any given approach. If one strategy does not seem to show much improvement, then a different one should be used. Because each student has individual needs, a teacher may need to utilize several different techniques tailored to the needs of each student.

To monitor student process, the following approaches should be considered:

- Asking questions in the classroom during and after a lecture
- Cultivating a classroom environment that encourages student questions
- Circulating around the classroom and engaging in one-on-one conferences during in-class assignments
- Giving periodic quizzes
- Leaving sufficient time for questions at the end of a lecture
- Assigning and collecting homework and returning the corrected material immediately
- Giving midterms and final exams
- Conducting regular reviews of student progress through the above methods and adjusting teaching strategies accordingly

Another strategy to assess student knowledge and identify areas in need of development is to create a K-W-L chart in preparation for a lesson that introduces a new topic. First, students are prompted for what they already know (K). Then, they are asked to consider what they want to know (W). The instructor may then choose to adjust the lesson by spending less time on areas that students are already proficient in and by spending more time on areas that students want to know more about. Finally, after the lesson, students can be asked to reflect on what they learned (L). A K-W-L chart lets students know that they are active participants in their own learning.

Using Effective Oral Communication

Identifying Techniques to Use in Collaborative Discussions
Effective oral communication requires the ability to express oneself clearly and diplomatically. It is imperative to teach students from a young age the value of respecting oneself and others, as well as the ability to keep an open mind during discussion and not to make things personal. Students should also be taught to keep the flow of discussion in alignment with the topic at hand and to listen actively as well as speak.

Age-appropriate Topics
Keeping topics *age-appropriate* is one way to stimulate productive conversation. It is important to consider the breadth of knowledge that an individual or group is likely to have. One of the primary objectives of conferencing in an academic setting is to challenge students into thinking critically. Choosing topics that are too advanced or beyond the realm of their knowledge would be an act in futility as they do not have the appropriate tools to engage in conversation. Similarly, topics that are too simple will not be beneficial as they will not be challenging. When choosing a topic, teachers should consider the average age of students, their vocabulary, their reading and writing skills, and life experiences they are likely to have.

Facilitating Appropriate Discussion Behavior
Once an appropriate topic has been chosen, discussions should be monitored to facilitate appropriate behavior. It is very important to stress that all perspectives will be welcome and respected and to make sure that student inquiries and responses are in alignment with that principle.

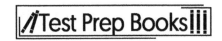

The following are suggestions for facilitating appropriate discussion behavior in a group setting:

1. Cultivating an environment of inclusion and mutual respect

    *   Students should introduce themselves and be encouraged to address each other by name. "Icebreaker" games are an effective way to get students to know each other before engaging in any discussions.

    *   Allowing enough time for students to think about the topic and thoughtfully contribute to the discussion will encourage inclusion.

    *   The use of insulting or disrespectful language, tone, or body language should not be permitted.

    *   Students should be made aware of differences in cultural and social perspectives.

    *   Students should be encouraged to be mindful of the language they are using.

    *   Teachers should not make assumptions on how students will respond or behave based on their cultural, racial, or religious backgrounds.

    *   Everyone should have a chance to speak—e.g., teachers should not show favoritism towards a particular student or set of students or allow more tenacious students to dominate the discussion.

    *   Particular perspectives or ideas should not be verbally or nonverbally discouraged. Instead, students should be encouraged to think critically about what is being discussed and what they are saying.

    *   It's important not to rush students or make any student feel as though his or her comments and ideas are not important.

    *   Facilitators should not display a sense of superiority.

2. Keeping discussions productive

    *   Teachers should be explicit about the expectations or goals of the discussion and guide students back towards the topic if they get off track.

    *   Demonstrating what disrespectful behavior looks like at the start of the discussion can help establish clear expectations. Students should be reminded not to take things personally or to identify with any emotions they may experience from the discussion and, instead, approach the topics with logic.

    *   Ideas or counterarguments should be related to personal experiences or backed with evidence. Students should validate each other's ideas first before arguing in a respectful way, such as "I respect what you are saying," or "I understand where you are coming from."

    *   Stereotyping and sweeping generalizations should be identified when used and subsequently avoided.

- If a student goes off on a tangent, he or she should be guided back to the primary topic or purpose by asking him/her to summarize what he/she is saying.

- If the discussion becomes heated or emotional, students should be encouraged to explore the real issue that is causing the emotions. The teacher might say, "I think there is a greater issue here that we should discuss openly and respectfully." Alternatively, students can be asked if they would like to take break and resume the discussion later. A teacher may also wish to bring up the differing values that are being displayed in the conference in an unbiased way so that students can recognize what they're truly arguing about.

- It's important that teachers avoid arguing with a student if the student attacks them. Acknowledging this kind of behavior only validates it.

3. Encouraging participants/guiding the flow of discussion

- For shy students, it's helpful to call on them by name and ask if they have any thoughts/feedback, while being nonjudgmental if they admit they don't know or don't have anything to say.

- Asking questions and requesting examples when students make a comment or present an idea helps guide the discussion flow.

- Writing student comments down and asking for other participants to elaborate on them will encourage more participation.

- Depending on the exercise, giving the students a topic or asking a student to present one will elicit participation.

- For students who have trouble participating in large groups, breaking up discussion into smaller groups will help them feel more comfortable.

Ensuring Accountability

One of the most challenging things about group discussions is ensuring that the students have prepared for it. For a discussion to be as productive as possible, students should be held accountable for completing their due preparation, such as homework, pre-class readings, or research. This can be done in numerous ways, such as by requiring the students to complete an at-home assignment and submit it electronically by midnight the previous night or on the day before. This assignment could be worth a significant grade to encourage students to complete it, and it could be in the following forms: responding to a question on an online discussion board, completing quizzes in reading comprehension, or answering true or false questions.

To ensure accountability during the discussion, students should be encouraged to participate by asking questions and asked to elaborate when something is unclear. Letting them take notes and leaving plenty of time for the formulation of thoughts and follow-up questions will increase accountability. After the discussion has ended, passing out a handout that students can fill out or having them summarize the discussion online are two beneficial strategies for accountability.

Evaluating the Effectiveness of Strategies for Effective Discussions

To increase student participation in discussion, teachers should consider the following strategies:

- Asking students what they know about the topic and writing their responses on the white or blackboard, which creates an outline of what the students do and don't know as well as increases their self-esteem.

- Having an anonymous question box where students can write down questions that can be read before or during the discussion, being careful not to react negatively to any questions, verbally or non-verbally, so as not to damage self-esteem

- Allowing students to teach each other, proven as the most effective way to learn something is to teach someone else what has been learned—e.g., writing their own tests or homework, conducting one-on-one conferences

- Dividing the class into smaller groups if students seem non-responsive, which helps shy students feel less intimidated and more comfortable in smaller settings

- Allowing students to work together, which encourages them to interact with others and allows them to feel more comfortable with doing so when it comes time for group discussion

- Asking students to create a topic to get them to initiate the conversation

- Using games to make the discussion fun and motivate students to participate

The effectiveness of these strategies will depend entirely on the class. Teachers should use the assessment tools discussed previously to determine whether the techniques have been effective and adjust the teaching style accordingly.

Many of the above strategies can be used for one-on-one discussions as well. The most important things to keep in mind in keeping a student engaged and comfortable during a one-on-one discussion are as follows:

- Asking follow-up questions
- Clarifying any unclear or obscure questions or statements
- Never making the student feel unintelligent or inadequate
- Being as reassuring as possible, particularly if a student expresses insecurity in his or her abilities
- Being patient and allowing time for the student to sort out thoughts and ask necessary questions

Understanding Students' Various Perspectives, Cultures, and Backgrounds

Planning Instruction Responsive to Students' Individual and Group Needs

It can be difficult as a teacher to be mindful of the varying individual and group identities present in the classroom. Every adult has internalized beliefs that he or she has learned through experience or was taught as a child. To encourage cultural understanding and dismantle stereotypes, an essential part of the curriculum should be devoted to teaching students tolerance of themselves and others.

One thing teachers should keep in mind is that although students may share similar group identities—race, nationality, socioeconomic status—they also contain differing individual identities. They may have different religions, different ancestry, or different languages. These differences will present themselves in everything the students do, from curricular activities, such as reading and writing, to social interaction in speaking and listening.

To incorporate cultural awareness into classroom instruction, the teacher must first express interest in the cultural backgrounds of his or her students. If the instructor is closed off against certain identities, the students will echo these viewpoints, being reserved in expression and also harboring the same reservations towards cultures different than their own. Therefore, the first step in planning instructions that tailors to the cultural needs of the students is to be interested in their identities. This can be done in many ways, but one sure way that a teacher can show he or she cares is by engaging in diversity activities, such as introduction cards or online questionnaires that students can fill out about themselves. These may include the following categories:

- Where they or their ancestors are from
- Their age
- Their primary and secondary languages, if applicable
- Their religious or spiritual beliefs
- Their race
- Their gender, what they identify as
- Any other information they feel comfortable introducing to the class

These are only a few examples of the information that can be gathered on index cards or questionnaires. Teachers can have the students go around the room and introduce themselves, while displaying curiosity about the backgrounds of their classmates. The information may then be kept throughout the year for reference and will also help the teacher collect a sort of census on the different cultural backgrounds their students possess.

Another proven way to show interest in the students and instill a sense of cultural awareness in the classroom is to assign a family survey project in which the students report on their heritage, the special customs or holidays that they practice in their home, the languages they speak, or anything they wish to share about their families and identities. These projects can be completed on PowerPoint presentations, poster boards, or video interviews, and students should be encouraged to bring items of cultural significance to share with their classmates.

The knowledge gained from these sorts of activities will greatly help the teacher to create a curriculum of instruction that encourages tolerance. For example, in reading about historic events involving horrendous crimes against a certain race or culture, teachers should try to read texts that contain both perspectives—e.g., texts from German, American, and Jewish voices related to the Holocaust. Discussions such as these can be taught in very compassionate and empathetic ways, while still recognizing the horrors of the crimes committed. Students can also consider historical and contemporary texts to see how perspectives have evolved on significant cultural issues throughout history.

It is also important to create a curriculum in which all students see themselves, their race, their genders, and their religions represented in their studies. The curriculum should not focus on the achievements of one particular group, such as only teaching history related to Christian Caucasian culture. Further, teachers should be ready and willing to alter the curriculum to respond to the needs of the students.

To instill a sense of tolerance in the classroom, students can complete worksheets on the kinds of behavior and diction that are acceptable when they encounter differences in cultures or belief systems. They can create a play or scene where they write out such an encounter and how they would approach it to build understanding between people from different backgrounds. Monitoring the interactions between the students and pointing out any situation or comment that unintentionally conveys intolerance will help make them more aware. Students should be educated on stereotypes. Most importantly, teachers should always lead by example by being as open and impartial as possible.

Strategies for Creating a Safe Environment

There are countless different strategies for creating a culturally-safe environment in which reading, writing, speaking, and listening can take place. First, the classroom should be clean and orderly to minimize distractions. It should reflect cultural diversity or impartiality. The classroom should be arranged with resources readily available and easily accessible so that a teacher never has to turn his or her back on their students. Secondly, the classroom should be arranged in a way that makes interaction with fellow students easy. The classroom environment also must convey a sense of emotional safety where students feel comfortable expressing themselves without fear of bullying or prejudice. This means teachers should be modeling respectful behavior for students, establishing rules of respectful interaction between students, and addressing any instances of disrespectful speech or behavior. Once the classroom has been set up safely, the following strategies are effective ways to incorporate cultural awareness into the curriculum:

- Reading
    - Choosing texts that reflect multicultural perspectives and include different cultures
    - Clarifying that chosen texts may contain culturally and racially-sensitive language and pointing out the intolerance in such texts—e.g., the excessive use of racial slurs in Mark Twain's Huckleberry Finn and what they suggested of cultural intolerance at the time
    - Trying not to choose texts that talk about an entire race or religion in general, but specific aspects of the race or religion to avoid sweeping generalizations or stereotypes about a group—e.g., choosing books on certain Native American tribes, rather than books solely on Native Americans, texts that offer specifics about a particular religion
    - Choosing texts that are both fun and serious, such as texts on cultural festivities and fun, as well as those about wars and hardships
    - Choosing texts that are historically accurate and up-to-date
    - If allowing students to choose their own books, encouraging them to explore texts that are culturally different than their own

- Writing
    - Requiring that students complete a project, such as a presentation or examination of a famous figure, who represents a culture or religion or philosophy that differs from their own
    - Monitoring student writing, checking for the presence of stereotypes and intolerance, and holding one-on-one conferences with students whenever concerns arise

- o Instructing students on the appropriate vocabulary, diction, and phrasing when writing on culturally or racially sensitive subjects

- o Encouraging students to write together via collaborative discussion boards, blogs, or group projects

- o Assigning students to groups with varying cultural, religious, racial, or socioeconomic backgrounds

- o Having students write on personal experiences where they have encountered intolerance against themselves or others

- • Speaking

  - o Holding frequent group discussions in which students can learn how to converse with people of different backgrounds, which may include inviting guest speakers

  - o Arranging chairs in circles or allowing students to remain at their desks in a way that demonstrates equality among all participants

  - o Monitoring student behavior during such discussions, calling attention to any inappropriate dialogue, use of stereotypes, or displays of intolerance the moment they occur

  - o Leading by example by treating all races, religions, cultures, genders and gender identities with tolerance and respect

  - o Beginning every discussion with a reminder to be accepting and tolerant of differing perspectives and beliefs and asserting that offensive language or behavior will not be tolerated

- • Listening

  - o Encouraging active listening by allowing students to take notes and ask questions

  - o Asking students to summarize what they heard

  - o Discouraging interruptions or non-verbal negative responses, such as eye-rolls, sighs, or noises of disgust, to reduce disrespectful behavior during discussion

  - o Allowing enough time for all students to speak so that others may listen and giving everyone an equal amount of time to speak without letting any one person dominate discussion

When an instructor is knowledgeable in a subject, demonstrates passion for the work, and creates an environment of respect, students will learn a great deal from him or her as a mentor, both in real-world situations and in academics.

Practice Questions

1. Which mode of writing aims to inform the reader objectively about a particular subject or idea and typically contains definitions, instructions, or facts within its subject matter?
   a. Argumentative
   b. Informative
   c. Narrative
   d. Descriptive

2. Editorials, letters of recommendation, and cover letters most likely incorporate which writing mode?
   a. Argumentative
   b. Informative
   c. Narrative
   d. Descriptive

3. The type of writing mode an author chooses to use is dependent on which of the following elements?
   a. The audience
   b. The primary purpose
   c. The main idea
   d. Both A and B

4. The rhetorical appeal that elicits an emotional and/or sympathetic response from an audience is known as which of the following?
   a. Logos
   b. Ethos
   c. Pathos
   d. None of the above

5. Which of the following refers to what an author wants to express about a given subject?
   a. Primary purpose
   b. Plot
   c. Main idea
   d. Characterization

6. Which organizational style is used in the following passage?

   There are several reasons why the new student café has not been as successful as expected. One factor is that prices are higher than originally advertised, so many students cannot afford to buy food and beverages there. Also, the café closes rather early; as a result, students go out in town to other late-night gathering places rather than meeting friends at the café on campus.

   a. Cause and effect order
   b. Compare and contrast order
   c. Spatial order
   d. Time order

7. Short, succinct sentences are best written for which of the following audiences?
a. Adults or people more familiar with a subject
b. Children or people less familiar a subject
c. Politicians and academics
d. University students

8. A student is starting a research assignment on Japanese-American internment camps during World War II, but she is unsure of how to gather relevant resources. Which of the following would be the most helpful advice for the student?
a. Conduct a broad internet search to get a wide view of the subject.
b. Consult an American history textbook.
c. Find websites about Japanese culture such as fashion and politics.
d. Locate texts in the library related to World War II in America and look for references to internment camps in the index.

9. Which of the following should be evaluated to ensure the credibility of a source?
a. The publisher, the author, and the references
b. The subject, the title, and the audience
c. The organization, stylistic choices, and transition words
d. The length, the tone, and the contributions of multiple authors

10. Which of the following is true of using citations in a research paper?
a. If a source is cited in the bibliography, it is not necessary to cite it in the paper as well.
b. In-text citations differ in format from bibliographic citations.
c. Students should learn one standard method of citing sources.
d. Books and articles need to be cited, but not websites or multimedia sources.

11. Which of the following is true regarding the integration of source material to maintain the flow of ideas in a research project or paper?
a. There should be at least one quotation or paraphrase in every paragraph.
b. If a source is paraphrased instead of being directly quoted, it is not necessary to include a citation.
c. An author's full name must be used in every signal phrase.
d. In-text citations should be used to support the paper's argument without overwhelming the student's writing.

12. Which citation style requires the inclusion of the author's last name, the title of the book or article, and its publication date in a bibliography entry?
a. MLA
b. APA
c. Chicago
d. All of the above

13. Which of the following qualities are necessary for effective speech delivery?
a. Knowledge, erudite vocabulary, and conviction
b. Charm, wit, and connection
c. Confidence, authenticity, and succinctness
d. Compassion, empathy, and tolerance

14. Which of the following components are advantageous and disadvantageous regarding the use of Microsoft PowerPoint presentations?
    a. They present information that can be taken home and reviewed later, but the audience may choose to read rather than listen.
    b. They allow the audience to follow along with the process of explaining difficult concepts and copy down their own version, but there is limited space that may need to be erased.
    c. They allow for pictures, words, and videos, but they can be distracting from the presence of the speaker.
    d. They allow for participants to interact with the physical world which helps solidify concepts, but they can be distracting if not properly introduced.

15. Which of the following should be considered before utilizing a technological device in the classroom?
    a. The age of the students
    b. Whether it is user friendly
    c. If it will be used in the real world
    d. All of the above

16. Which of the following refers to a teaching strategy in which two or more students work together to develop a project, work through an idea, or solve a problem?
    a. Listening
    b. Collaborative learning
    c. Active learning
    d. Discussion

17. A method of learning in which the student learns through physical interaction with an object is referred to as which of the following?
    a. Auditory Learning
    b. Visual Learning
    c. Kinesthetic Learning
    d. Distance Learning

18. Which of the following defines the stage of writing that involves adding to, removing, rearranging, or re-writing sections of a piece?
    a. The revising stage
    b. The publishing stage
    c. The writing stage
    d. The pre-writing stage

19. A research-proven approach to teaching writing that involves a short lesson, independent writing time, and sharing is known as which of the below?
    a. Writing workshop
    b. Teacher modeling
    c. The writer's notebook
    d. Freewriting

20. Which of the following is true regarding the most effective methods of teaching the writing process?
    a. Instruction should be standardized so that all students should learn writing in the same way.
    b. Feedback should be generalized, giving overall instruction for improvement instead of focusing on certain aspects of writing.
    c. The most important way a student learns is by doing, so they should be given as many opportunities to write as possible.
    d. Students should be compared to one another, so lower-achieving students can model their writing skills on those of more proficient students.

21. Which of the following is true of assessing student writing?
    a. Students should only be given positive feedback so as not to make them feel discouraged.
    b. Students should engage in peer assessments without instructor interference, to increase independent writing skills.
    c. Writing assessments should always be holistic so students get the "big picture" of effective writing.
    d. Writing assessments should be returned in a timely manner.

22. Which of the following is an evaluation tool that explicitly states the expectations of an assignment and breaks it down into components and evaluation criteria?
    a. A one-on-one conference
    b. An analytic rubric
    c. A verbal feedback session
    d. A discussion with peers

23. When it comes to class discussions, setting guidelines for the discussion, preventing distracting tangents, and refraining from arguing with students are examples of which of the following?
    a. Cultivating an environment of inclusion and mutual respect
    b. Keeping discussions productive
    c. Encouraging participation
    d. Ensuring accountability

24. If student participation in discussion is low, which of the following should be done to encourage more active participation?
    a. Divide the classroom into smaller groups so that shy students will feel more comfortable speaking up.
    b. Brainstorm ideas related to the topic on the board.
    c. Allow students to lead discussion or suggest topics.
    d. All of the above

25. Which of the following is NOT a strategy used to foster cultural awareness in the classroom?
    a. Creating introduction cards that contain student background information
    b. Assigning a family heritage project
    c. Grouping students based on their backgrounds
    d. Creating lessons related to important historic events in diverse cultures

Answer Explanations

1. B: The key word here is "inform," which is the primary purpose of all informative modes. They contain facts, definitions, instructions, and other elements with the objective purpose of informing a reader— such as study guides, instruction manuals, and textbooks. Choice A is incorrect because an argumentative mode contains language that is subjective and is intended to persuade or to inform with a persuasive bias. Choice C is incorrect as a narrative mode is used primarily to tell a story and has no intention of informing, nor is the language inherently objective. Choice D is incorrect as descriptive modes possess no inherent intent to inform, and are used primarily to describe.

2. A: Editorials, recommendation letters, and cover letters all seek to persuade a reader to agree with the author, which reflects an argumentative mode. Choice B is incorrect because the intent of the above examples is to persuade a reader to agree with the author, not to present information. Choice C is incorrect as the above examples are not trying to tell a story. Choice D is also incorrect because while the above examples may contain many descriptions, that is not their primary purpose.

3. D: Both the audience and primary purpose are important for choosing a writing mode. The audience is an important factor as the diction, tone, and stylistic choices of a written piece are tailored to fit the audience demographic. The primary purpose is the reason for writing the piece, so the mode of writing must be tailored to the most effective delivery method for the message. Choice A is incorrect because it only takes into account one of the aspects for choosing a mode and the audience, but leaves out the primary purpose. Choice B is incorrect for the same reason, except it only takes into account the primary purpose and forgets the audience. Choice C is incorrect as the main idea is the central theme or topic of the piece, which can be expressed in any form the author chooses. Because the mode depends on the reason the author wrote the piece, the main idea is not an important factor in determining which mode of writing to use.

4. C: Pathos is the rhetorical appeal that draws on an audience's emotions and sympathies. Choice A is incorrect as logos appeals to the audience's logic, reason, and rational thinking, using facts and definitions. Choice B is incorrect because ethos appeals to the audience's sense of ethics and moral obligations. Choice D is incorrect because C contains the correct answer; thus, the answer cannot be "None of the above."

5. C: The main idea of a piece is its central theme or subject and what the author wants readers to know or understand after they read. Choice A is incorrect because the primary purpose is the reason that a piece was written, and while the main idea is an important part of the primary purpose, the above elements are not developed with that intent. Choice B is incorrect because while the plot refers to the events that occur in a narrative, organization, tone, and supporting details are not used only to develop plot. Choice D is incorrect because characterization is the description of a person.

6. A: The passage describes a situation and then explains the causes that led to it. Also, it utilizes cause and effect signal words, such as *causes, factors, so,* and *as a result*. B is incorrect because a compare and contrast order considers the similarities and differences of two or more things. C is incorrect because spatial order describes where things are located in relation to each other. Finally, D is incorrect because time order describes when things occurred chronologically.

7. B: Children and less educated audiences tend to understand short, succinct sentences more effectively because their use helps increase information processing. Choice A is incorrect as longer, more fluid sentences are best used for adults and more educated audiences because they minimize processing times and allow for more information to be conveyed. Choices C and D are incorrect because there is no correlation between a given profession and a writing style; rather, it depends on how familiar the audience is with a given subject.

8. D: Relevant information refers to information that is closely related to the subject being researched. Students might get overwhelmed by information when they first begin researching, so they should learn how to narrow down search terms for their field of study. Both Choices A and B are incorrect because they start with a range that is far too wide; the student will spend too much time sifting through unrelated information to gather only a few related facts. Choice C introduces a more limited range, but it is not closely related to the topic that is being researched. Finally, Choice D is correct because the student is choosing books that are more closely related to the topic and is using the index or table of contents to evaluate whether the source contains the necessary information.

9. A: The publisher, author, and references are elements of a resource that determine credibility. If the publisher has published more than one work, the author has written more than one piece on the subject, or the work references other recognized research, the credibility of a source will be stronger. Choice B is incorrect because the subject and title may be used to determine relevancy, not credibility, and the audience does not have much to do with the credibility of a source. Choice C is incorrect because the organization, stylistic choices, and transition words are all components of an effectively-written piece, but they have less to do with credibility, other than to ensure that the author knows how to write. The length and tone of a piece are a matter of author's preference, and a work does not have to be written by multiple people to be considered a credible source.

10. B: In-text citations are much shorter and usually only include the author's last name, page numbers being referenced, and for some styles, the publication year. Bibliographic citations contain much more detailed reference information. B is incorrect because citations are necessary both in the text and in a bibliography. C is incorrect because there are several different citation styles depending on the type of paper or article being written. Rather, students should learn when it is appropriate to apply each different style. D is incorrect because all sources need to be cited regardless of medium.

11. D: The purpose of integrating research is to add support and credibility to the student's ideas, not to replace the student's own ideas altogether. Choice A is incorrect as the bulk of the paper or project should be comprised of the author's own words, and quotations and paraphrases should be used to support them. Outside sources should be included when they enhance the writer's argument, but they are not required in every single paragraph. Choice B is also incorrect because regardless of whether ideas are directly quoted or paraphrased, it is essential to always credit authors for their ideas. The use of the author's full name in every signal phrase is unnecessary, so Choice C is also incorrect.

12. D: Although there are differences between each formatting style, they all include the same basic components listed in the question for bibliography entries—the author's name, the title of the work, and its publication date. Therefore, the correct answer is all of the above.

13. C: Confidence, authenticity, and succinctness are the most important aspects of speech delivery as they instill trust in the audience and deliver a message succinctly, which reduces the likelihood that the audience's attention will wander. Choice A is incorrect as knowledge is important for a good speech, as is conviction, but appropriate vocabulary depends on the audience. The message could get lost if vocabulary is inappropriate or unfamiliar to the audience. Choice B is incorrect because though charm, wit, and connection could be useful, charming people may also be perceived as inauthentic and lose

credibility with their audience. Choice *D* is incorrect because though compassion, empathy, and tolerance are all good qualities in a person and work well in certain speech topics, they are not inherent qualities that one must possess to deliver a good speech.

14. C: Microsoft PowerPoint is the medium that can present pictures, words, and videos because of its inherent digital format, but the vastness of the projection and presence of information can distract an audience from the presence of the speaker. Choice *A* is incorrect because handouts are print mediums that present information that can be taken home and reviewed later, and participants can choose to read rather than listen. Choice *B* is incorrect because blackboards, whiteboards, and overhead projectors allow for students to follow along with processes, but provide limited space. Choice *D* is incorrect because physical objects allow for participants to interact with the physical world, but they can be distracting if not properly introduced.

15. D: The age of the students is an important aspect to consider when using technology because many devices have basic requirements for motor and comprehension skills. User friendliness is important as not all students have the same amount of technological literacy. Teaching students to use a device that they will never use again is futile, so it's more practical to use technology that they will use in the real world. Choice *D* is the correct answer because it includes all of these aspects; Choices *A*, *B*, and *C* are incorrect because they only include one of the above aspects.

16. B: Collaborative learning is defined as a teaching strategy is which two or more students work together to learn something new. Choice *A* is incorrect because listening is not a teaching strategy so much as a learning strategy, and listening is required for most types of learning. Choice *C* is incorrect because active learning is when a student learns by doing, either by teaching another student or writing a summary. Two or more students coming together to learn actively, as opposed to one instructing the other, is more indicative of collaborative learning. Choice *D* is incorrect because although discussions may occur with two or more students, it does not usually include any form of active learning, such as creating a project or solving a problem.

17. C: One component of kinesthetic learning is students learning through physical interaction with something, such as a model or an interactive computer simulation. Choice *A* is incorrect as auditory learning is when a student learns through listening, such as listening to a lecture on a podcast. Choice *B* is incorrect because visual learning occurs when a student learns through watching or observing, such as an instructional video. Choice *D* is incorrect because distance learning occurs when the teacher and student are not in the same place and is achieved through technological means.

18. A: The revising stage involves adding, removing, and rearranging sections of a written work. Choice *B* is incorrect as the publishing stage involves the distribution of the finished product to the publisher, teacher, or reader. Choice *C* is incorrect because the writing stage is the actual act of writing the work, and generally does not including editing or revision. Choice *D* is incorrect as the pre-writing stage involves the planning, drafting, and researching of the intended piece.

19. A: The writing workshop is the teaching strategy involving a short lesson on how to write or to give the topic, an individual writing session, and then a sharing section in which the students read what they have written and listens to others. Choice *B* is incorrect because teacher modeling means being an example from which the students can imitate their writing and behavior. It requires that teachers be skilled writers themselves. Choice *C* is incorrect because the writer's notebook is the physical or digital notebook where students write and store their work. And Choice *D* is incorrect because freewriting refs to giving students a set length of time to write on a subject without editing their ideas or expressions.

20. C: Giving the students many opportunities to write is the most effective way they learn to write, and the most effective learning occurs through doing. Choice *A* is incorrect because instruction should not be standardized; it should be individualized to fit different students' needs. Choice *B* is incorrect because feedback should be specific, not generalized, so that a student may focus on the parts of his or her writing that need work, while also recognizing what he or she is doing well in other areas. Choice *D* is incorrect because though it can be helpful for students to evaluate and discuss each other's work, it is important to avoid creating a culture of comparison and competition in the classroom, which can lead to lower morale and negatively affect relationships between students.

21. D: Writing assessments should be conducted and returned in a timely manner so that students can learn from their mistakes, which in turn helps them to avoid repeating the same errors and developing ineffective writing habits. Choice *A* is incorrect because though it is important to present criticism in a constructive and encouraging way, it is better to integrate positive feedback with suggestions for improvement. Choice *B* is incorrect because peer review can be an effective learning tool, but only when it is properly modeled and monitored by the instructor. Choice *C* is incorrect because, although a holistic approach is one way to approach writing assessments, it is not the only useful method; in some cases, students need to focus on one specific area of improvement.

22. B: An analytic rubric is an evaluation tool that explicitly states the expectations of an assignment and breaks it down into components. Choice *A* is incorrect because a conference is a discussion, not a tool. Choice *C* is incorrect because although verbal feedback may accompany a completed rubric, it is not the tool itself. Choice *D* is incorrect because a discussion with peers is not a tool, though it may incorporate evaluation.

23. B: Keeping discussions productive means that the instructor guides the flow of discussion to ensure adherence to the topic, which would entail preventing tangents and not engaging with the student should they wish to argue. Choice *A* is incorrect because cultivating an environment of inclusion and mutual respect involves letting everyone have a chance to speak, monitoring student behavior for respect and tolerance, and educating students on cultural differences. Choice *C* is incorrect because encouraging participation involves galvanizing the students by calling on them, writing their responses on the board, or having them create their own topic. Choice *D* is incorrect because ensuring accountability requires that students prepare for class participation by doing homework or taking quizzes, etc. and are held accountable by being assigned or deducted points.

24. D: Dividing students into smaller groups allows for shy students who are intimidated by a large group of people to feel more comfortable in participating. Allowing students to lead discussion or suggest topics gives them more responsibility while also encouraging them to prepare more for class and letting them choose topics that they are interested in. Brainstorming ideas together can give students a starting point when they do not feel confident or knowledgeable about speaking up on a topic. Therefore, *D*—all of the above—is the best answer.

25. C: As a non-example, *C* is correct because rather than grouping students based on shared backgrounds, instructors will offer more learning opportunities by encouraging them to interact with those from backgrounds that are different from their own. Creating introduction cards that contain the students' cultural background is a very enlightening way to get to know the students and demonstrate interest in them so they may feel compelled to mirror an instructor's interest and display curiosity

towards others. Likewise, assigning family heritage projects encourage the students to examine their culture and then learn about other cultures in a safe and tolerant environment. Choice *D* is incorrect because it is another example of a strategy that allows students to expand their cultural knowledge.

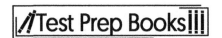

Dear Praxis English Language Arts Test Taker,

We would like to start by thanking you for purchasing this study guide for your Praxis English Language Arts exam. We hope that we exceeded your expectations.

Our goal in creating this study guide was to cover all of the topics that you will see on the test. We also strove to make our practice questions as similar as possible to what you will encounter on test day. With that being said, if you found something that you feel was not up to your standards, please send us an email and let us know.

We would also like to let you know about other books in our catalog that may interest you.

Praxis II Elementary Education Test

This can be found on Amazon: amazon.com/dp/162845847X

Praxis II Social Studies

amazon.com/dp/1628457686

Praxis Core Study Guide

amazon.com/dp/1628457899

We have study guides in a wide variety of fields. If the one you are looking for isn't listed above, then try searching for it on Amazon or send us an email.

Thanks Again and Happy Testing!
Product Development Team
info@studyguideteam.com

Interested in buying more than 10 copies of our product? Contact us about bulk discounts:
bulkorders@studyguideteam.com

FREE Test Taking Tips DVD Offer

To help us better serve you, we have developed a Test Taking Tips DVD that we would like to give you for FREE. **This DVD covers world-class test taking tips that you can use to be even more successful when you are taking your test.**

All that we ask is that you email us your feedback about your study guide. Please let us know what you thought about it – whether that is good, bad or indifferent.

To get your **FREE Test Taking Tips DVD**, email freedvd@studyguideteam.com with "FREE DVD" in the subject line and the following information in the body of the email:

  a. The title of your study guide.

  b. Your product rating on a scale of 1-5, with 5 being the highest rating.

  c. Your feedback about the study guide. What did you think of it?

  d. Your full name and shipping address to send your free DVD.

If you have any questions or concerns, please don't hesitate to contact us at freedvd@studyguideteam.com.

Thanks again!

Made in the USA
Las Vegas, NV
21 March 2021